# Contents

**4** YOUR JOURNAL
Make the most of this book

**6** CHAPTER ONE
Crown • Mini Wave • Wave

**32** CHAPTER TWO
Triangle • Scale • Target

**58** CHAPTER THREE
Square • House • Stingray

**84** CHAPTER FOUR
Bowtie • Mirrored Triangles • Trial by Triangles

**110** CHAPTER FIVE
Zigzag • Bunting • Spider Web

**136** CHAPTER SIX
Cross • This way or That way • Compass

**162** QUESTIONS
How did you get on?

**163** DOWNLOADS
Handy downloadable layouts

---

First published in Great Britain by DJ Murphy Publishers Ltd in 2023
DJ Murphy (Publishers) Ltd, Olive Studio, Grange Road, Farnham, Surrey GU10 2DQ
www.djmurphy.co.uk

Text copyright © DJ Murphy Publishers Ltd 2023
All rights reserved. No part of this publication may be reproduced or transmitted in any form or by any means without prior written authority from DJ Murphy (Publishers) Ltd.

Written by Tania Grantham
Edited by Halima Crabtree, Nicky Moffatt
Designed by Sarah Garland, Adam Witt
Photography by Jon Stroud
Managing Director Zoe Cannon
Commercial Director Abi Cannon
Printed by Cambrian printers
ISBN 978-1-913787-20-2

# HOW TO USE YOUR JOURNAL

This book contains a year's worth of polework exercises. There are six full layouts, each of which has a series of three stages that progressively build towards the full layout. I suggest you set out every stage for a week to 10 days and use it three to five times. Progress like this through all three stages, so you have a total of 21–30 days for each series.

For every stage of the layout series, there are three full sessions of exercises. Work though each session, then combine the exercises if you use the stage again within the week to 10 days when it's laid out. Remember, polework is more strenuous than normal schooling, so make sure you give your horse variety, including hacking and rest days, between sessions.

**For each session, there is a series of journal questions, including:**
- date of writing in journal?
- how many times did you ride each exercise?
- how hard did you find the session?
- what did the session make you focus on most in terms of your aiding/riding?
- what did the session make you focus on most in terms of your horse's responses and way of going?
- what would you most like to improve in your schooling for next time?

Once you have worked through all six series over six months, go back to the first one and do them all again over the next six months. Again, there are journal questions for the second time you use them, including:
- date?
- did you find it easier or harder than the first time?
- if this has changed, why do you think it's changed?
- how would you like to improve it next time?

Of course, you can come back to the layouts again and again, and keep your own records. There are also many more ways to use the layouts than I've been able to fit into this book. Continue experimenting and you will have many years of use from them.

# ABOUT
## *you and your horse*

Name..................................................................................................................................

Horse's name.....................................................................................................................


What would you most like to improve in your riding?
..........................................................................................................................................
..........................................................................................................................................
..........................................................................................................................................
..........................................................................................................................................
..........................................................................................................................................
..........................................................................................................................................
..........................................................................................................................................

What would you most like to improve in your horse's way of going?
..........................................................................................................................................
..........................................................................................................................................
..........................................................................................................................................
..........................................................................................................................................
..........................................................................................................................................
..........................................................................................................................................

What is your horse's stride length?
Place three poles in a straight line, five heel-to-toe steps apart and try riding over it in trot. Is it comfortable? If not, try four or six heel-to-toe steps. What striding is best for your horse?

CHAPTER ONE

# Wave

**CROWN • MINI WAVE • WAVE**

This series is about straightness and having your horse genuinely between both legs and reins. I use this layout for all levels of horse, with the youngsters, it's great for teaching them to be more upright. With the advanced horses, it's a useful test and reminder to have them correctly aligned.

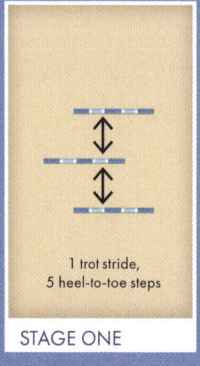

1 trot stride,
5 heel-to-toe steps

**STAGE ONE**

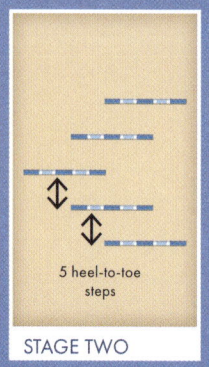

5 heel-to-toe steps

**STAGE TWO**

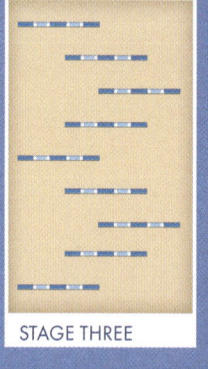

**STAGE THREE**

# THE CROWN
## *Session one*

**SET UP**
- start on the centre line, with the poles lying parallel to the short side
- overlap the poles by two thirds
- set the poles out one stride apart, as explained in the about you and your horse section on page five

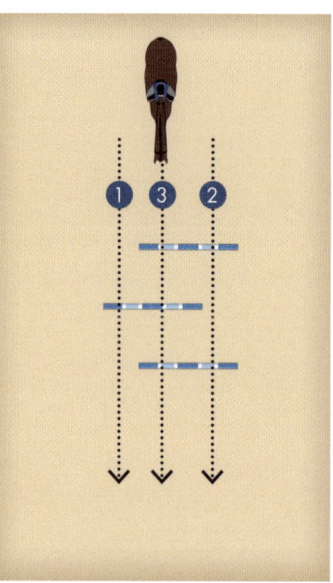

**STRAIGHT LINES**
**In trot**
1. Trot over one pole, having the horse upright between both legs and reins so he doesn't fall out to the side.
2. Trot over two poles.
3. Trot over all three poles, focusing on the alignment as the horse has to work harder over all three poles.

**In canter**
1. Canter over the single pole on a straight line.
2. Canter over two poles on a straight line.

**SESSION QUESTIONS: FIRST USE**

Date of writing in journal?......................................................................

How many times did you ride each exercise? ........................................

How hard did you find the session?

😃   😐   😩

What did this session make you focus on most in terms of your aiding/riding?

...........................................................................................................
...........................................................................................................
...........................................................................................................
...........................................................................................................
...........................................................................................................

# Stage one

Two of your horse's trot strides should be exactly the same distance as one canter stride.

What did this session make you focus on most in terms of your horse's responses and way of going?

..................................................................................................................................................
..................................................................................................................................................
..................................................................................................................................................
..................................................................................................................................................

What would you most like to improve in your schooling for next time?

..................................................................................................................................................
..................................................................................................................................................
..................................................................................................................................................
..................................................................................................................................................

## SESSION QUESTIONS: FIRST USE

Date of writing in journal?.....................................................................................

How many times did you ride each exercise? ...............................................

How hard did you find the session?

😃        😐        😩

What did this session make you focus on most in terms of your aiding/riding?

.....................................................................................................................

.....................................................................................................................

.....................................................................................................................

.....................................................................................................................

.....................................................................................................................

# Stage one

# THE CROWN
*Session two*

**DIAGONAL LINES**
- in trot, ride a diagonal line over two poles, thinking about making a balanced turn from the long side and riding forwards over the poles
- establish canter, turn off the long side, ride a trot transition before the poles, trot over the poles, then canter on the other lead after the poles. Focus on keeping the line the same as it was without the transitions

**Level 1:** ride the transitions in the corners, to help with bend and correct strike off.

**Level 2:** ride the transitions either side of the poles on the straight line. Clearly position your body before you ask for the strike off.

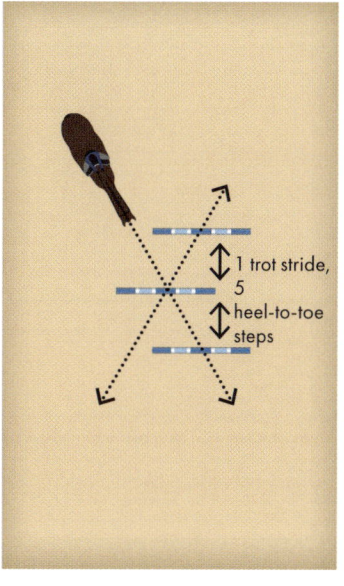

1 trot stride, 5 heel-to-toe steps

What did this session make you focus on most in terms of your horse's responses and way of going?

..................................................................................................................
..................................................................................................................
..................................................................................................................

What would you most like to improve in your schooling for next time?

..................................................................................................................
..................................................................................................................
..................................................................................................................

# THE CROWN
*Session three*

**TRANSITIONS**
- ride straight between the poles, in walk, trot and canter
- ride transitions between the poles; for example, walk, halt at X, walk
- get creative with transitions, for example...
– trot, walk, trot
– canter, trot, canter
– trot, halt, trot
– canter, walk, canter
– trot, halt, rein back, trot

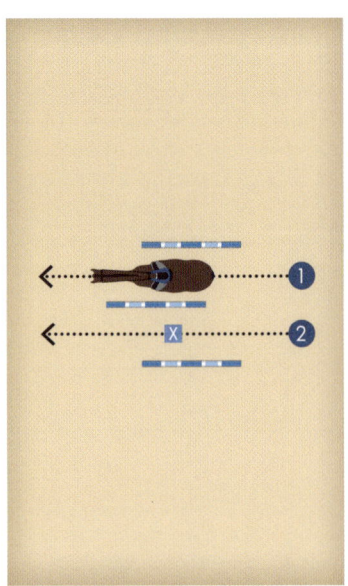

## "Poles encourage straightness and accuracy to your transitions"

**SESSION QUESTIONS: FIRST USE**

Date of writing in journal?..................................................

How many times did you ride each exercise? ..................................

How hard did you find the session?

😀  😐  😩

What did this session make you focus on most in terms of your aiding/riding?

..........................................................................
..........................................................................
..........................................................................
..........................................................................

Stage one

What did this session make you focus on most in terms of your horse's responses and way of going?

..................................................................................................................................
..................................................................................................................................
..................................................................................................................................
..................................................................................................................................

What would you most like to improve in your schooling for next time?

..................................................................................................................................
..................................................................................................................................
..................................................................................................................................
..................................................................................................................................

Date .............................................. Session ........................................................

Did you find it easier or harder than the first time? ........................................................

If this has changed, why do you think it has changed?

..............................................................................................................................
..............................................................................................................................
..............................................................................................................................

How would you like to improve it next time?

..............................................................................................................................
..............................................................................................................................
..............................................................................................................................

Date .............................................. Session ........................................................

Did you find it easier or harder than the first time? ........................................................

If this has changed, why do you think it has changed?

..............................................................................................................................
..............................................................................................................................
..............................................................................................................................

How would you like to improve it next time?

..............................................................................................................................
..............................................................................................................................
..............................................................................................................................

**THINK ABOUT...** WHAT HAS CHANGED | YOUR AIDS

## Stage one

Date .................................................Session ...............................................................

Did you find it easier or harder than the first time?.........................................................

If this has changed, why do you think it has changed?

..............................................................................................................................................
..............................................................................................................................................
..............................................................................................................................................

How would you like to improve it next time?

..............................................................................................................................................
..............................................................................................................................................
..............................................................................................................................................

**NOTES**

..............................................................................................................................................
..............................................................................................................................................
..............................................................................................................................................
..............................................................................................................................................
..............................................................................................................................................
..............................................................................................................................................
..............................................................................................................................................
..............................................................................................................................................
..............................................................................................................................................
..............................................................................................................................................
..............................................................................................................................................

| YOUR HORSE'S RESPONSE | YOUR HORSE'S WAY OF GOING

# MINI WAVE
*Session one*

**SET UP**
- overlap poles by two-thirds and measure both ends so each pole is parallel
- this is best set up on the centre line so you have more room to ride around the poles

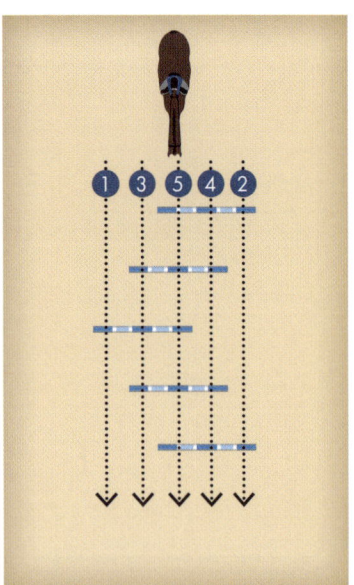

**STRAIGHT LINES**
**In trot**
1. Trot over one pole.
2. Trot over two poles.
3. Trot over three poles.
4. Trot over four poles.
5. Trot over all five poles.

**In canter**
1. Canter over one pole.
2. Canter over two poles.

**SESSION QUESTIONS: FIRST USE**

Date of writing in journal? ...........................................................................................

How many times did you ride each exercise? ...........................................................

How hard did you find the session?

😀　　😐　　😧

What did this session make you focus on most in terms of your aiding/riding?

................................................................................................................................

................................................................................................................................

................................................................................................................................

................................................................................................................................

Stage two

As before, work over different numbers of poles concentrating on using both legs and reins to keep your horse lined up. Use the stripes on the poles as guidelines to stay straight.

What did this session make you focus on most in terms of your horse's responses and way of going?

..................................................................................................................................

..................................................................................................................................

..................................................................................................................................

..................................................................................................................................

What would you most like to improve in your schooling for next time?

..................................................................................................................................

..................................................................................................................................

..................................................................................................................................

..................................................................................................................................

### SESSION QUESTIONS: FIRST USE

Date of writing in journal?..................................................................................

How many times did you ride each exercise? ...................................................

How hard did you find the session?

😃   😐   😩

What did this session make you focus on most in terms of your aiding/riding?

..................................................................................................................

..................................................................................................................

..................................................................................................................

..................................................................................................................

..................................................................................................................

Stage two

# MINI WAVE
*Session two*

**DIAGONAL LINES**
Just as you did with the crown, ride diagonal lines in trot, this time over three poles on the diagonal.

If you vary the angle that you ride, it will slightly change the distance between the poles. Line two will encourage the horse to lengthen more than line one.

Focus on making a balanced turn from the long side, while maintaining a consistent tempo in the trot. Horses have limited vision at close range, by crossing the poles at an angle they will find the distance harder to judge so will tend to be more active and try harder to clear them, resulting in bigger, more expressive paces.

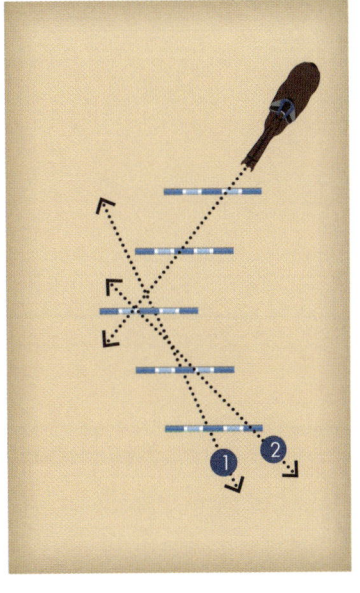

> "This exercise creates bigger, more expressive paces"

What did this session make you focus on most in terms of your horse's responses and way of going?

..................................................................................................................
..................................................................................................................
..................................................................................................................
..................................................................................................................

What would you most like to improve in your schooling for next time?

..................................................................................................................
..................................................................................................................
..................................................................................................................
..................................................................................................................

19

# MINI WAVE
*Session three*

**CIRCLES**
1. Starting on a straight line, ride a circle around the poles going over the single pole at the halfway point of the circle. Start in trot, then try it in canter.
**Add in transitions**
- trot the circle, walk before the pole and over the pole, trot on again on the circle after the pole
- canter the circle, trot before the pole, over the pole and canter again on the circle after the pole

2. Starting on a straight line, ride two individual circles going over the two poles at the halfway points of the circles. Ride this exercise in trot, but if you want to take it to the next level try canter.
**Add in transitions**
- trot the circle, walk before the pole and over the pole, trot on again on the circle after the pole
- canter the circle, trot before the pole, over the pole and canter again on the circle after the pole

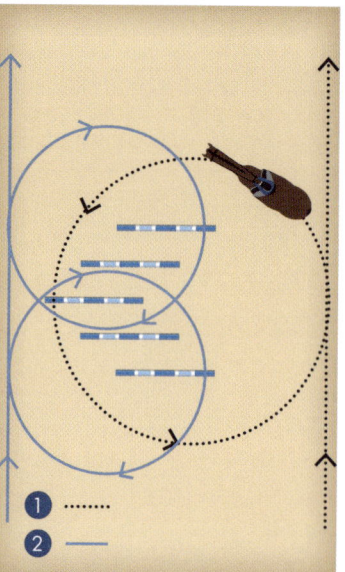

**SESSION QUESTIONS: FIRST USE**

Date of writing in journal?..................................................................

How many times did you ride each exercise? ..............................................

How hard did you find the session?

😃    😐    😩

What did this session make you focus on most in terms of your aiding/riding?

..................................................................................................
..................................................................................................
..................................................................................................
..................................................................................................
..................................................................................................

Stage two

What did this session make you focus on most in terms of your horse's responses and way of going?

..................................................................................................................................................
..................................................................................................................................................
..................................................................................................................................................
..................................................................................................................................................

What would you most like to improve in your schooling for next time?

..................................................................................................................................................
..................................................................................................................................................
..................................................................................................................................................
..................................................................................................................................................

Date .................................Session ...............................................................

Did you find it easier or harder than the first time?.................................................

If this has changed, why do you think it has changed?
..................................................................................................................................
..................................................................................................................................
..................................................................................................................................

How would you like to improve it next time?
..................................................................................................................................
..................................................................................................................................
..................................................................................................................................

Date .................................Session ...............................................................

Did you find it easier or harder than the first time?.................................................

If this has changed, why do you think it has changed?
..................................................................................................................................
..................................................................................................................................
..................................................................................................................................

How would you like to improve it next time?
..................................................................................................................................
..................................................................................................................................
..................................................................................................................................

**THINK ABOUT... WHAT HAS CHANGED | YOUR AIDS**

# Stage two

Date ................................Session ...................................................

Did you find it easier or harder than the first time?......................................................

If this has changed, why do you think it has changed?
..........................................................................................................
..........................................................................................................
..........................................................................................................

How would you like to improve it next time?
..........................................................................................................
..........................................................................................................
..........................................................................................................

**NOTES**
..........................................................................................................
..........................................................................................................
..........................................................................................................
..........................................................................................................
..........................................................................................................
..........................................................................................................
..........................................................................................................
..........................................................................................................
..........................................................................................................
..........................................................................................................
..........................................................................................................

| YOUR HORSE'S RESPONSE | YOUR HORSE'S WAY OF GOING

# WAVE
*Session one*

**SET UP**
As before, overlap poles by two thirds and measure both ends of each pole to keep them all parallel. Stand at A or C to check you can achieve a straight line down the centre of the layout over all nine poles.

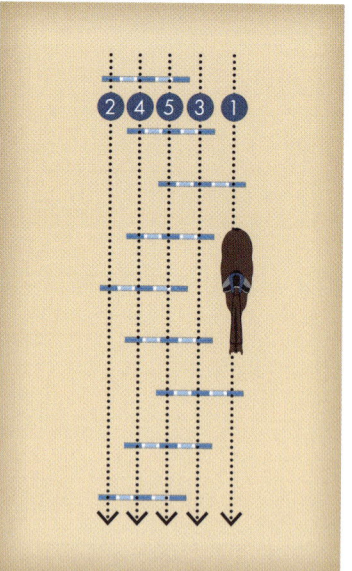

**STRAIGHT LINES**
Work in trot over different numbers of poles, just as you did with the Crown and Mini Wave layouts. However, this will now be harder for your horse, as not only are there more poles for him to step over, but the gaps between vary in the number of steps he'll need to take.
1. Trot over two poles.
2. Trot over three poles.
3. Trot over six poles.
4. Trot over seven poles.
5. Trot over nine poles.

**SESSION QUESTIONS: FIRST USE**

Date of writing in journal?..................................................................

How many times did you ride each exercise? ..............................................

How hard did you find the session?

😀     😐     😫

What did this session make you focus on most in terms of your aiding/riding?

..............................................................................

..............................................................................

..............................................................................

..............................................................................

Stage three

As the rider, focus on the line you want to ride as your horse may try to drift to avoid really having to push from behind.

What did this session make you focus on most in terms of your horse's responses and way of going?

..................................................................................................................................
..................................................................................................................................
..................................................................................................................................
..................................................................................................................................

What would you most like to improve in your schooling for next time?

..................................................................................................................................
..................................................................................................................................
..................................................................................................................................
..................................................................................................................................

### SESSION QUESTIONS: FIRST USE

Date of writing in journal?..................................................................................

How many times did you ride each exercise? ..................................................

How hard did you find the session?

😀        😐        😩

What did this session make you focus on most in terms of your aiding/riding?

..................................................................................................................................
..................................................................................................................................
..................................................................................................................................
..................................................................................................................................
..................................................................................................................................

Stage three

# WAVE
*Session two*

**TRANSITIONS**

Any transition can be ridden in the gaps between the poles. Look at dressage tests for ideas of the sorts of transitions you will be asked to perform on a straight line or serpentine lines. For example, at Elementary you are asked to ride simple changes on a serpentine.

For more progressive transitions, walk a half circle to the gap between poles two and three. Ride a trot transition as you enter the gap between the poles and from trot to canter as you exit, canter a loop around poles three to seven, before trotting through the poles. Finish by transitioning to walk and riding another half circle.

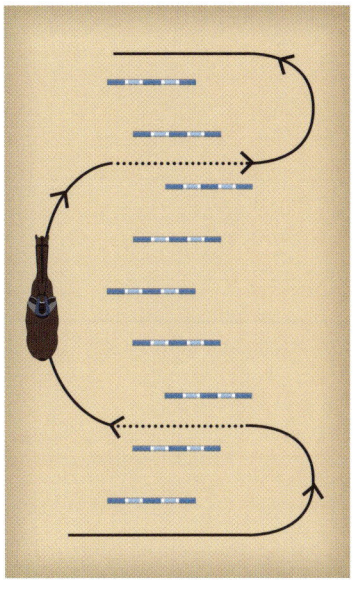

## "Use the gaps in the poles to work on straightness and the placement of the transitions"

What did this session make you focus on most in terms of your horse's responses and way of going?

..................................................................................................................................
..................................................................................................................................
..................................................................................................................................
..................................................................................................................................

What would you most like to improve in your schooling for next time?

..................................................................................................................................
..................................................................................................................................
..................................................................................................................................
..................................................................................................................................

27

# WAVE
*Session three*

**CURVED LINE**
In trot, ride a slightly curved line over all nine poles. Riding a curve while crossing the poles is a huge test of alignment and control.
- keep the curve very shallow and gradual
- think of using your upper legs to steer the saddle and your horse's shoulders, while remaining level with your hips and shoulders
- focus on the poles where you will need to ask your horse to change from one bend to the other
- as you and your horse grow in confidence, you can start to amplify each of the curves

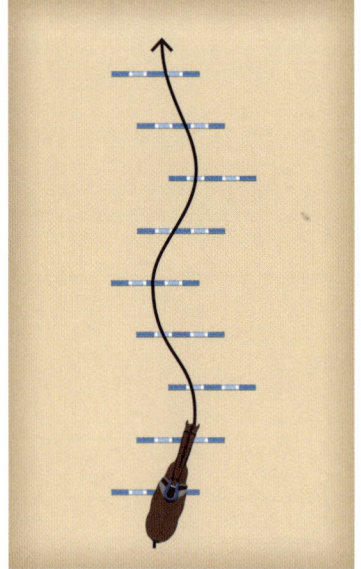

## "This is the ultimate test of alignment and control"

**SESSION QUESTIONS: FIRST USE**

Date of writing in journal?..................................................................................

How many times did you ride each exercise? ............................................

How hard did you find the session?

😃     😐     😥

What did this session make you focus on most in terms of your aiding/riding?

..........................................................................................................................

..........................................................................................................................

..........................................................................................................................

..........................................................................................................................

..........................................................................................................................

Stage three

What did this session make you focus on most in terms of your horse's responses and way of going?
..................................................................................................................
..................................................................................................................
..................................................................................................................
..................................................................................................................

What would you most like to improve in your schooling for next time?
..................................................................................................................
..................................................................................................................
..................................................................................................................
..................................................................................................................

Date ..................................Session ........................................................................

Did you find it easier or harder than the first time?......................................................

If this has changed, why do you think it has changed?

..................................................................................................................................
..................................................................................................................................
..................................................................................................................................

How would you like to improve it next time?

..................................................................................................................................
..................................................................................................................................
..................................................................................................................................

Date ..................................Session ........................................................................

Did you find it easier or harder than the first time?......................................................

If this has changed, why do you think it has changed?

..................................................................................................................................
..................................................................................................................................
..................................................................................................................................

How would you like to improve it next time?

..................................................................................................................................
..................................................................................................................................
..................................................................................................................................

**THINK ABOUT... WHAT HAS CHANGED | YOUR AIDS**

## Stage three

Date .................................................Session ........................................................................

Did you find it easier or harder than the first time?......................................................................

If this has changed, why do you think it has changed?
................................................................................................................................................
................................................................................................................................................
................................................................................................................................................

How would you like to improve it next time?
................................................................................................................................................
................................................................................................................................................
................................................................................................................................................

**NOTES**
................................................................................................................................................
................................................................................................................................................
................................................................................................................................................
................................................................................................................................................
................................................................................................................................................
................................................................................................................................................
................................................................................................................................................
................................................................................................................................................
................................................................................................................................................
................................................................................................................................................
................................................................................................................................................

| YOUR HORSE'S RESPONSE | YOUR HORSE'S WAY OF GOING

CHAPTER TWO

# Target

## TRIANGLE • SCALE • TARGET

This series is very versatile but will particularly help you focus on turns and circles. The exercises will help to increase suppleness and manoeuvrability of your horse, while making you focus on your aiding. There are plenty of options to increase the difficulty as your horse becomes more advanced.

STAGE ONE

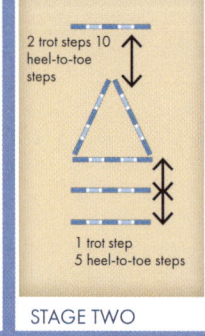

STAGE TWO

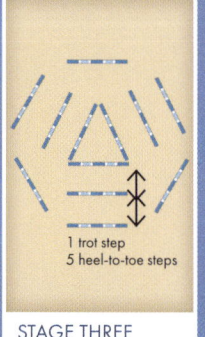

STAGE THREE

# TRIANGLE
*Session one*

> **SET UP**
> Build your triangle on the centre line so the point is directed towards A or C and X is in the centre.

**STRAIGHT LINES**
In walk and trot, ride a straight line through the triangle. Enter over the centre stripe of the pole at the base of the triangle and ride out over the point. To make the exercise harder, ride in through the point and out via the base.
- focus on riding balanced turns from the long side and back to the opposite long side, using your aids to keep your horse upright
- most horses will tend to want to drift in one direction, so, to help control that, use your upper leg and close it against the knee roll, making sure you keep your hands even each side of your horse's neck
- you can ride this exercise in canter, making sure you sit up and keep your horse in a good balanced canter

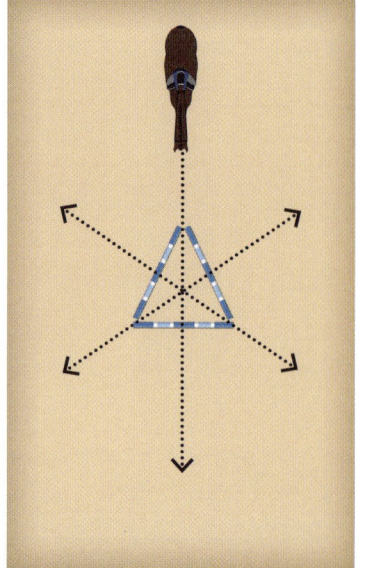

> **SESSION QUESTIONS: FIRST USE**

Date of writing in journal?..............................................................................

How many times did you ride each exercise? ...............................................

How hard did you find the session?

😃   😐   😩

What did this session make you focus on most in terms of your aiding/riding?

..................................................................................................................
..................................................................................................................
..................................................................................................................
..................................................................................................................
..................................................................................................................

Stage one

What did this session make you focus on most in terms of your horse's responses and way of going?

.................................................................................................................
.................................................................................................................
.................................................................................................................
.................................................................................................................

What would you most like to improve in your schooling for next time?

.................................................................................................................
.................................................................................................................
.................................................................................................................
.................................................................................................................

## SESSION QUESTIONS: FIRST USE

Date of writing in journal?..................................................................................

How many times did you ride each exercise? ............................................

How hard did you find the session?

😃     😐     😩

What did this session make you focus on most in terms of your aiding/riding?

..................................................................................................................

..................................................................................................................

..................................................................................................................

..................................................................................................................

..................................................................................................................

Stage one

# TRIANGLE
*Session two*

**CIRCLES**
Ride 20m circles over the triangle, making sure you practise the circle on both reins. Horses are naturally one-sided, meaning most horses will have one rein on which they tend to fall in, while, on the other, they tend to fall out. The poles are a great way to highlight and improve this.
- think about the size of the circle either side of the poles, so you ride from long side to long side (assuming the arena is 20m)
- use the stripes on the poles to check that your circle is symmetrical
- as you're on a circle, you will be crossing the poles at an angle, not perpendicular

**Key**
Middle = walk (black)
Inside third = trot one step (blue)
Outside third = trot two steps or one canter (red)

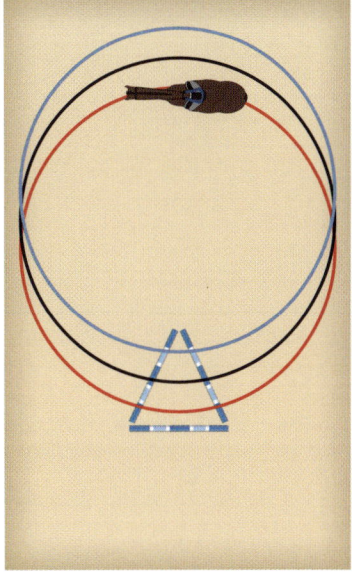

What did this session make you focus on most in terms of your horse's responses and way of going?

..................................................................................................................................
..................................................................................................................................
..................................................................................................................................
..................................................................................................................................

What would you most like to improve in your schooling for next time?

..................................................................................................................................
..................................................................................................................................
..................................................................................................................................
..................................................................................................................................

37

# TRIANGLE
*Session three*

**TRANSITIONS**

Add in transitions before and after the poles. You can do this on a straight line or a circle. For example, approach in trot, walk before the poles, walk over the poles, trot after. Also canter–trot–canter, canter–walk–canter.

- if you're riding a straight line through the triangle, you can also ride a change of rein, so change your lead when cantering
- focus on making sure the line or circle doesn't change as you add in transitions

Having the poles not only helps the rider with accuracy but also tends to make transitions more reactive, as your horse is naturally more engaged having stepped over the poles. These transitions are often found in dressage tests and they are there to test accuracy, obedience, balance and control.

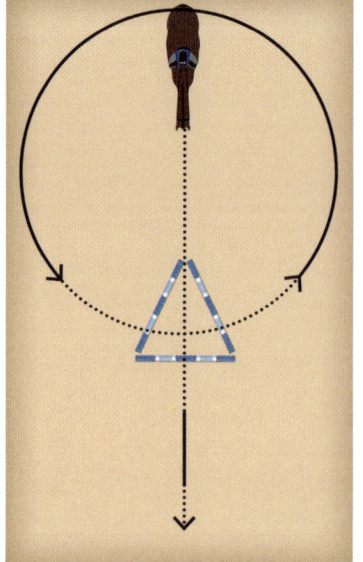

## SESSION QUESTIONS: FIRST USE

Date of writing in journal?..................................................................................

How many times did you ride each exercise? ..............................................

How hard did you find the session?

😀    😐    😩

What did this session make you focus on most in terms of your aiding/riding?

..........................................................................................................................

..........................................................................................................................

..........................................................................................................................

..........................................................................................................................

Stage one

What did this session make you focus on most in terms of your horse's responses and way of going?

..................................................................................................................................................
..................................................................................................................................................
..................................................................................................................................................
..................................................................................................................................................

What would you most like to improve in your schooling for next time?

..................................................................................................................................................
..................................................................................................................................................
..................................................................................................................................................
..................................................................................................................................................

Date .........................................Session ............................................................

Did you find it easier or harder than the first time?.......................................................

If this has changed, why do you think it has changed?

..........................................................................................................................................

..........................................................................................................................................

..........................................................................................................................................

How would you like to improve it next time?

..........................................................................................................................................

..........................................................................................................................................

..........................................................................................................................................

Date .........................................Session ............................................................

Did you find it easier or harder than the first time?.......................................................

If this has changed, why do you think it has changed?

..........................................................................................................................................

..........................................................................................................................................

..........................................................................................................................................

How would you like to improve it next time?

..........................................................................................................................................

..........................................................................................................................................

..........................................................................................................................................

**THINK ABOUT... WHAT HAS CHANGED | YOUR AIDS**

## Stage one

Date .................................................Session ...............................................................

Did you find it easier or harder than the first time?...........................................................

If this has changed, why do you think it has changed?
...............................................................................................................................
...............................................................................................................................
...............................................................................................................................

How would you like to improve it next time?
...............................................................................................................................
...............................................................................................................................
...............................................................................................................................

**NOTES**

...............................................................................................................................
...............................................................................................................................
...............................................................................................................................
...............................................................................................................................
...............................................................................................................................
...............................................................................................................................
...............................................................................................................................
...............................................................................................................................
...............................................................................................................................
...............................................................................................................................
...............................................................................................................................

| YOUR HORSE'S RESPONSE | YOUR HORSE'S WAY OF GOING

# SCALE
*Session one*

**SET UP**
Building on the last layout, set this up on the centre line, adding the extra poles either side of the triangle. Use the distance that you worked out at the start of the book to measure your distances.

**STRAIGHT LINES**
Approach in trot and ride over the two poles and into the base of the triangle, then out over the point, and continue over the single pole. Then do it the other way round – single pole, point to base of triangle and out over the two poles.

This is fantastic centre line practice. Focus on your turns onto and off the centre line, and staying straight in a forward trot over the poles.

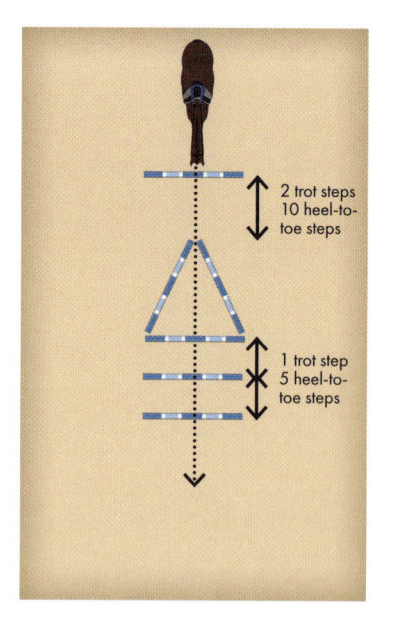

2 trot steps
10 heel-to-toe steps

1 trot step
5 heel-to-toe steps

**SESSION QUESTIONS: FIRST USE**

Date of writing in journal? ..................................................................................

How many times did you ride each exercise? ..................................................

How hard did you find the session?

😃    😐    😩

What did this session make you focus on most in terms of your aiding/riding?

..........................................................................................................................
..........................................................................................................................
..........................................................................................................................
..........................................................................................................................
..........................................................................................................................

Stage two

What did this session make you focus on most in terms of your horse's responses and way of going?

..................................................................................................................................
..................................................................................................................................
..................................................................................................................................
..................................................................................................................................

What would you most like to improve in your schooling for next time?

..................................................................................................................................
..................................................................................................................................
..................................................................................................................................
..................................................................................................................................

### SESSION QUESTIONS: FIRST USE

Date of writing in journal?......................................................................................

How many times did you ride each exercise? ..........................................................

How hard did you find the session?

😃   😐   😩

What did this session make you focus on most in terms of your aiding/riding?

..................................................................................................................................

..................................................................................................................................

..................................................................................................................................

..................................................................................................................................

..................................................................................................................................

Stage two

# SCALE
*Session two*

**CIRCLES THROUGH THE GAPS**
As with session two for the Triangle, think about the accuracy of the entire circle, making sure you continue to ride a curved line though the gap between the poles.

To level up the exercise, add in transitions either side of the gap; for example, canter the circle, trot through the gap and pick up canter again after. Use the gap to help hone your accuracy in the placement of the transitions.

> "Circles are a fundamental shape in dressage. Marks are awarded not just for the quality of the pace but also accuracy"

What did this session make you focus on most in terms of your horse's responses and way of going?

..................................................................................................................................
..................................................................................................................................
..................................................................................................................................
..................................................................................................................................

What would you most like to improve in your schooling for next time?

..................................................................................................................................
..................................................................................................................................
..................................................................................................................................
..................................................................................................................................

# SCALE
## *Session three*

**DOGLEG TURNS**
Start on the centre line and trot over the middle of the first pole. Then, ride a curved line so you cross the second pole slightly to the side and then go out over the side of the triangle. Try the exercise on both reins, riding a right curve and a left curve.

To level up the exercise, ride it in reverse, so enter through the side of the triangle and ride out over the two poles.

Focus on making a smooth turn and planning ahead. Horses can't react instantly to the aid you give while they are going over poles – they need warning to then respond in the next stride. Think about the difference between driving a car and the level of planning ahead that's required when driving a horsebox.

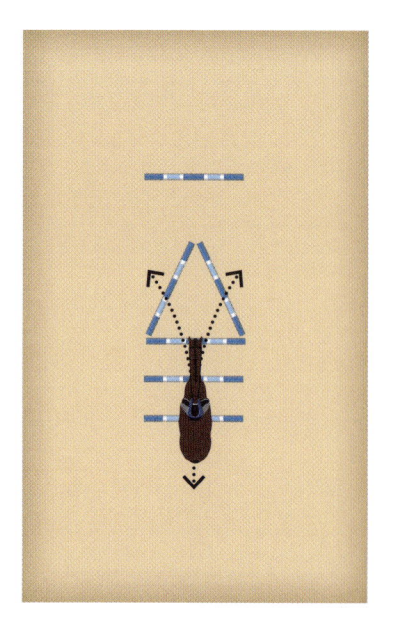

### SESSION QUESTIONS: FIRST USE

Date of writing in journal?....................................................................................

How many times did you ride each exercise? ................................................

How hard did you find the session?

😀     😐     😩

What did this session make you focus on most in terms of your aiding/riding?

........................................................................................................................................

........................................................................................................................................

........................................................................................................................................

........................................................................................................................................

........................................................................................................................................

46

Stage two

What did this session make you focus on most in terms of your horse's responses and way of going?
..................................................................................................................................................
..................................................................................................................................................
..................................................................................................................................................
..................................................................................................................................................

What would you most like to improve in your schooling for next time?
..................................................................................................................................................
..................................................................................................................................................
..................................................................................................................................................
..................................................................................................................................................

Date ..................................Session ..............................................................

Did you find it easier or harder than the first time?..................................................

If this has changed, why do you think it has changed?

..............................................................................................................................
..............................................................................................................................
..............................................................................................................................

How would you like to improve it next time?

..............................................................................................................................
..............................................................................................................................
..............................................................................................................................

Date ..................................Session ..............................................................

Did you find it easier or harder than the first time?..................................................

If this has changed, why do you think it has changed?

..............................................................................................................................
..............................................................................................................................
..............................................................................................................................

How would you like to improve it next time?

..............................................................................................................................
..............................................................................................................................
..............................................................................................................................

**THINK ABOUT...** WHAT HAS CHANGED | YOUR AIDS

# Stage two

Date ............................................Session ...........................................................................

Did you find it easier or harder than the first time?......................................................

If this has changed, why do you think it has changed?

..............................................................................................................................

..............................................................................................................................

..............................................................................................................................

How would you like to improve it next time?

..............................................................................................................................

..............................................................................................................................

..............................................................................................................................

**NOTES**

..............................................................................................................................

..............................................................................................................................

..............................................................................................................................

..............................................................................................................................

..............................................................................................................................

..............................................................................................................................

..............................................................................................................................

..............................................................................................................................

..............................................................................................................................

..............................................................................................................................

..............................................................................................................................

..............................................................................................................................

| YOUR HORSE'S RESPONSE | YOUR HORSE'S WAY OF GOING

# TARGET
*Session one*

### SET UP
This layout builds on the scale – adding in six additional poles. If you are setting it up from scratch, start in the centre of the arena with X in the middle of the triangle.

### STRAIGHT LINES
Ride straight lines through the gaps, using the poles to guide straightness. Ride through in walk, trot and canter.
Add in transitions,
- trot–walk–trot
- trot–halt–trot
- canter–trot–canter
- canter–walk–canter

**Next level**
If you have established flying changes, ride your changes through the gaps.

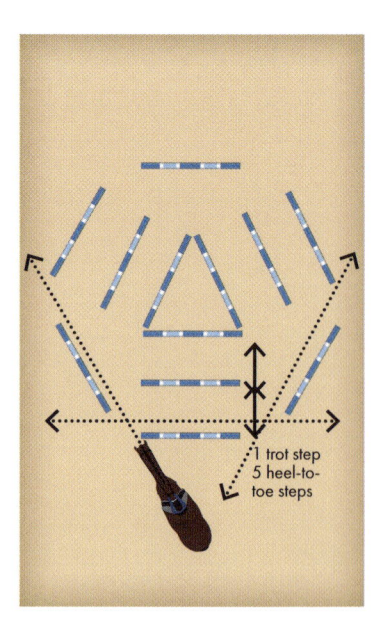

*1 trot step*
*5 heel-to-toe steps*

### SESSION QUESTIONS: FIRST USE

Date of writing in journal?....................................................................................

How many times did you ride each exercise? ......................................................

How hard did you find the session?

😃   😐   😩

What did this session make you focus on most in terms of your aiding/riding?

..........................................................................................................................
..........................................................................................................................
..........................................................................................................................
..........................................................................................................................
..........................................................................................................................

50

Stage three

What did this session make you focus on most in terms of your horse's responses and way of going?
..................................................................................................................................
..................................................................................................................................
..................................................................................................................................
..................................................................................................................................

What would you most like to improve in your schooling for next time?
..................................................................................................................................
..................................................................................................................................
..................................................................................................................................
..................................................................................................................................

**SESSION QUESTIONS: FIRST USE**

Date of writing in journal?......................................................................................

How many times did you ride each exercise? .............................................

How hard did you find the session?

😀    😐    😩

What did this session make you focus on most in terms of your aiding/riding?

..............................................................................................................................
..............................................................................................................................
..............................................................................................................................
..............................................................................................................................
..............................................................................................................................

Stage three

# TARGET
*Session two*

**DOGLEG TURNS**
Start by trotting over the centre of the first pole. Ride a curved line over the corner of the triangle and out over the poles. As with the dogleg over the Scale layout, focus on planning your turn and giving clear aids to your horse with enough warning for them to react.

By riding these turns over the poles, you are encouraging your horse to really stretch through the outside of his body. This is essential for achieving correct bend. The poles will also encourage lift and freedom within the horse's body, particularly the outside shoulder.

> "Give clear aids to your horse with enough time for him to react"

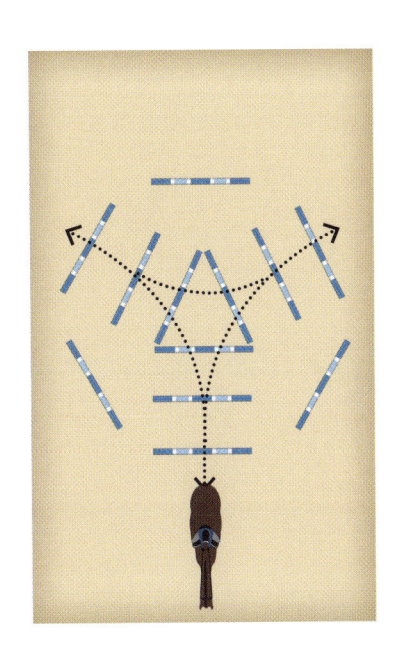

What did this session make you focus on most in terms of your horse's responses and way of going?

..................................................................................................................................

..................................................................................................................................

..................................................................................................................................

..................................................................................................................................

What would you most like to improve in your schooling for next time?

..................................................................................................................................

..................................................................................................................................

..................................................................................................................................

..................................................................................................................................

53

# TARGET
*Session three*

**SPIRAL WITH TRANSITIONS**
Start between the triangle and first set of poles in walk (black). After a circuit, move out to the gap between the two sets of poles and pick up trot (blue). Then after a circuit, move out to just around the outside of the poles and pick up your canter (red).

Focus on riding a continuously curving line, even when asking for transitions. The exercise can also be performed in reverse with downward transitions. Start outside the poles in canter, spiral into the gap between the poles and pick up trot, then go to walk as you spiral around the triangle.

**Next level**
To build on the exercise, make your transitions direct. Start around the triangle in walk and as you spiral out to the gap between the poles, pick up canter. Then perform in reverse with downward transitions. Start in canter and canter a circuit between the poles, then spiral in around the triangle and pick up walk.

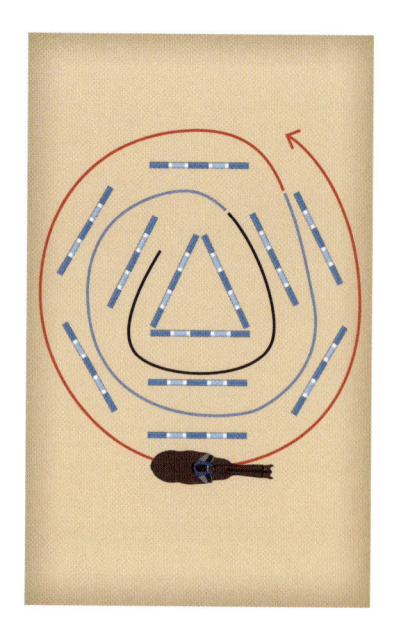

---

**SESSION QUESTIONS: FIRST USE**

Date of writing in journal?........................................................................

How many times did you ride each exercise? ...........................................

How hard did you find the session?

😃      😐      😩

What did this session make you focus on most in terms of your aiding/riding?

................................................................................................................
................................................................................................................
................................................................................................................
................................................................................................................
................................................................................................................

## Stage three

What did this session make you focus on most in terms of your horse's responses and way of going?

..................................................................................................................................
..................................................................................................................................
..................................................................................................................................
..................................................................................................................................

What would you most like to improve in your schooling for next time?

..................................................................................................................................
..................................................................................................................................
..................................................................................................................................
..................................................................................................................................

55

Date .................................................Session ................................................................................

Did you find it easier or harder than the first time?......................................................

If this has changed, why do you think it has changed?

.............................................................................................................................................

.............................................................................................................................................

.............................................................................................................................................

How would you like to improve it next time?

.............................................................................................................................................

.............................................................................................................................................

.............................................................................................................................................

Date .................................................Session ................................................................................

Did you find it easier or harder than the first time?......................................................

If this has changed, why do you think it has changed?

.............................................................................................................................................

.............................................................................................................................................

.............................................................................................................................................

How would you like to improve it next time?

.............................................................................................................................................

.............................................................................................................................................

.............................................................................................................................................

**THINK ABOUT...** WHAT HAS CHANGED | YOUR AIDS

## Stage three

Date .................................................Session .........................................................................

Did you find it easier or harder than the first time?..........................................................

If this has changed, why do you think it has changed?
..............................................................................................................................................
..............................................................................................................................................
..............................................................................................................................................

How would you like to improve it next time?
..............................................................................................................................................
..............................................................................................................................................
..............................................................................................................................................

**NOTES**

..............................................................................................................................................
..............................................................................................................................................
..............................................................................................................................................
..............................................................................................................................................
..............................................................................................................................................
..............................................................................................................................................
..............................................................................................................................................
..............................................................................................................................................
..............................................................................................................................................
..............................................................................................................................................
..............................................................................................................................................

| YOUR HORSE'S RESPONSE | YOUR HORSE'S WAY OF GOING

CHAPTER THREE

# Stingray

## SQUARE • HOUSE • STINGRAY

This is one of my all-time favourite layouts. It is designed to help you focus on test patterns and lines. Using poles for shapes is a fantastic way to work on accuracy and symmetry. The poles provide a guide for you to assess and monitor the line you are riding. It's amazing how many riders think they are riding accurately until they have the poles there, which then highlight that they're not. Working over the poles will encourage your horse to be more active from behind, improving their balance. This, in turn, will make your job easier.

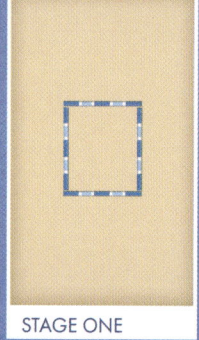

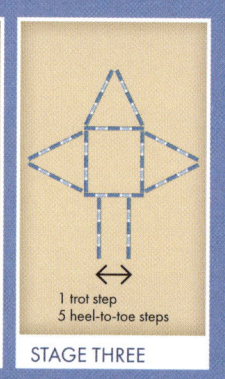

STAGE ONE

STAGE TWO

1 trot step
5 heel-to-toe steps

STAGE THREE

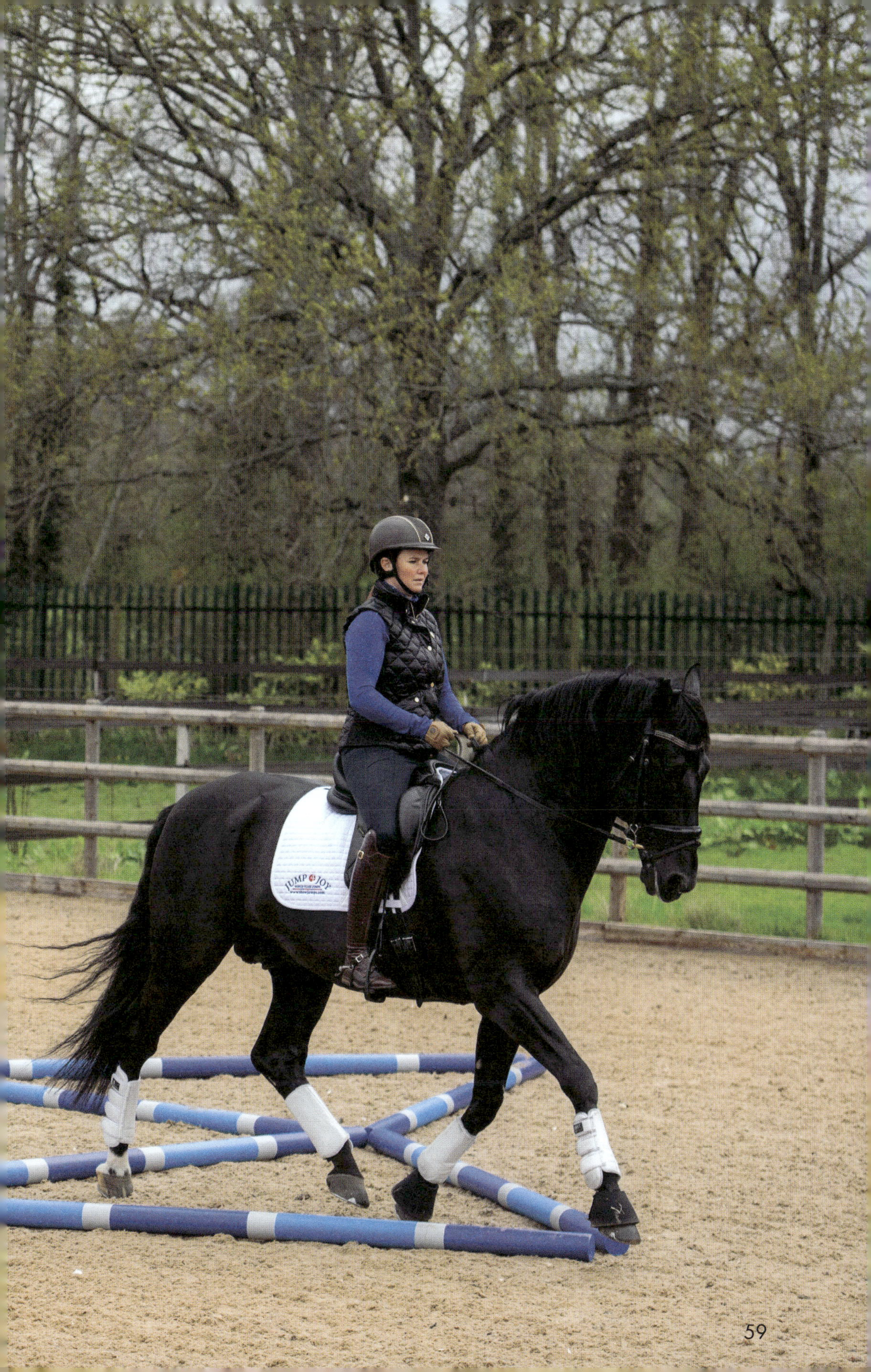
JUMP JOY

# SQUARE
*Session one*

### SET UP
Build this layout in the centre of the arena so the centre line runs through the middle of the square.

**STRAIGHT LINES**

Focus on riding good turns before and after the poles, using the stripes on the poles to help maintain straightness. In the walk, your horse will get 2–3 strides in the square. Experiment with different walks, medium, extended, etc.

In trot, they should get two strides in, but they might try to squeeze in three little steps. If they do this, think of swinging the trot forwards while maintaining balance to allow them to find the confidence to open out in the trot.

In the canter, it rides as a bounce. Focus on staying upright with your upper body and half-halt to encourage the horse to stay in an uphill balance. You want your horse to push from behind and bounce over the poles, as opposed to rushing and running over them.

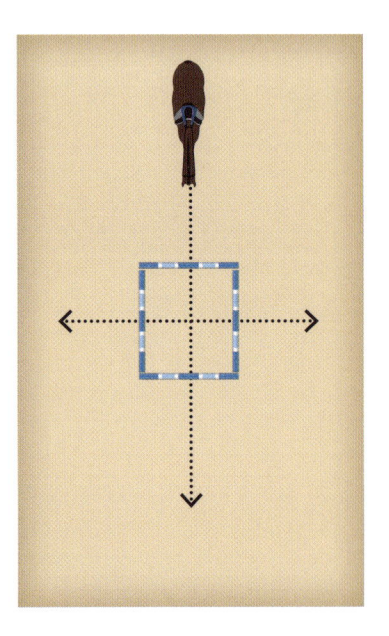

### SESSION QUESTIONS: FIRST USE

Date of writing in journal?......................................................................................

How many times did you ride each exercise? ...........................................................

How hard did you find the session?

😀    😐    😩

What did this session make you focus on most in terms of your aiding/riding?

..................................................................................................................

..................................................................................................................

..................................................................................................................

..................................................................................................................

..................................................................................................................

Stage one

What did this session make you focus on most in terms of your horse's responses and way of going?

..............................................................................................................................................
..............................................................................................................................................
..............................................................................................................................................
..............................................................................................................................................

What would you most like to improve in your schooling for next time?

..............................................................................................................................................
..............................................................................................................................................
..............................................................................................................................................
..............................................................................................................................................

### SESSION QUESTIONS: FIRST USE

Date of writing in journal?..................................................................................

How many times did you ride each exercise? ............................................

How hard did you find the session?

😃     😐     😩

What did this session make you focus on most in terms of your aiding/riding?

..................................................................................................................................

..................................................................................................................................

..................................................................................................................................

..................................................................................................................................

..................................................................................................................................

Stage one

# SQUARE
*Session two*

**DIAGONAL LINES**
You can ride these lines in walk and trot.
- make a balanced turn from the long side and look ahead to your line
- aim to stay straight through both points of the square

As you're going towards a small target, you may need to widen and lower your hands to help maintain straightness. Use your upper legs and think of keeping the saddle straight. Some horses may rush to avoid straightness, others will try to stop or move to the side, rather than going directly over the point. Approach in a slower pace initially, and talk to your horse to encourage him. Once he's confident, ride forward over the poles.

What did this session make you focus on most in terms of your horse's responses and way of going?

..................................................................................................................................
..................................................................................................................................
..................................................................................................................................
..................................................................................................................................

What would you most like to improve in your schooling for next time?

..................................................................................................................................
..................................................................................................................................
..................................................................................................................................
..................................................................................................................................

# SQUARE
## *Session three*

**TRANSITIONS**
Add in transitions either side of the square, for example...
- trot–walk–trot (black and blue)
- canter–trot–canter (red and black)

Any combination of transitions can be done on both the straight lines and the diagonal lines. For ideas, have a look at tests at the level you are aiming for.

Be aware of your own horse's tendency to drift and then pre-emptively correct it. For example, if you know they tend to drift right, keep your right upper leg and right elbow closed. It may even be necessary to over-correct and slightly flex your horse right to keep the shoulder upright and maintain straightness.

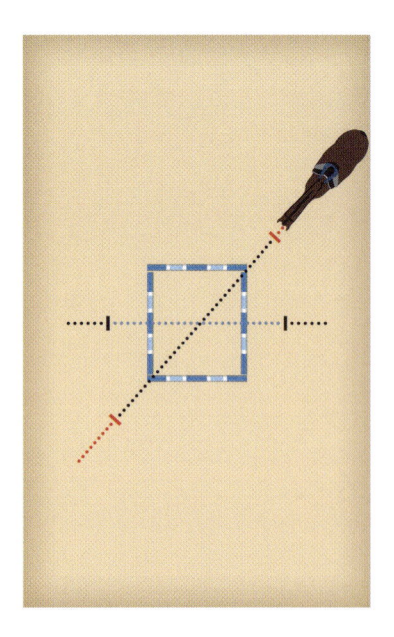

### SESSION QUESTIONS: FIRST USE

Date of writing in journal?....................................................................................

How many times did you ride each exercise? ............................................................

How hard did you find the session?

😀  😐  😩

What did this session make you focus on most in terms of your aiding/riding?

........................................................................................................................

........................................................................................................................

........................................................................................................................

........................................................................................................................

........................................................................................................................

Stage one

What did this session make you focus on most in terms of your horse's responses and way of going?

..................................................................................................................................................
..................................................................................................................................................
..................................................................................................................................................
..................................................................................................................................................

What would you most like to improve in your schooling for next time?

..................................................................................................................................................
..................................................................................................................................................
..................................................................................................................................................
..................................................................................................................................................

Date .............................................Session ..........................................................

Did you find it easier or harder than the first time?......................................................

If this has changed, why do you think it has changed?

..............................................................................................................................

..............................................................................................................................

..............................................................................................................................

How would you like to improve it next time?

..............................................................................................................................

..............................................................................................................................

..............................................................................................................................

Date .............................................Session ..........................................................

Did you find it easier or harder than the first time?......................................................

If this has changed, why do you think it has changed?

..............................................................................................................................

..............................................................................................................................

..............................................................................................................................

How would you like to improve it next time?

..............................................................................................................................

..............................................................................................................................

..............................................................................................................................

**THINK ABOUT...** WHAT HAS CHANGED | YOUR AIDS

## Stage one

Date ....................................Session ........................................................

Did you find it easier or harder than the first time?.......................................

If this has changed, why do you think it has changed?
...............................................................................................................
...............................................................................................................
...............................................................................................................

How would you like to improve it next time?
...............................................................................................................
...............................................................................................................
...............................................................................................................

**NOTES**
...............................................................................................................
...............................................................................................................
...............................................................................................................
...............................................................................................................
...............................................................................................................
...............................................................................................................
...............................................................................................................
...............................................................................................................
...............................................................................................................
...............................................................................................................
...............................................................................................................

| YOUR HORSE'S RESPONSE | YOUR HORSE'S WAY OF GOING

# THE HOUSE
## *Session one*

**SET UP**
Position the layout in the middle of the arena with the triangle pointing along the centre line towards A or C.

**STRAIGHT LINES THROUGH THE SQUARE**
Start by riding in over the central stripe of the square and out over the point of the triangle. To level up the exercise, ride it the other way around – in through the triangle and out of the square. Focus on making good, balanced turns onto and off the centre line.

Your horse will gain more lift and power over the poles in trot. Encourage them to maintain this after the poles with half-halts, active legs and the tempo of your rising.

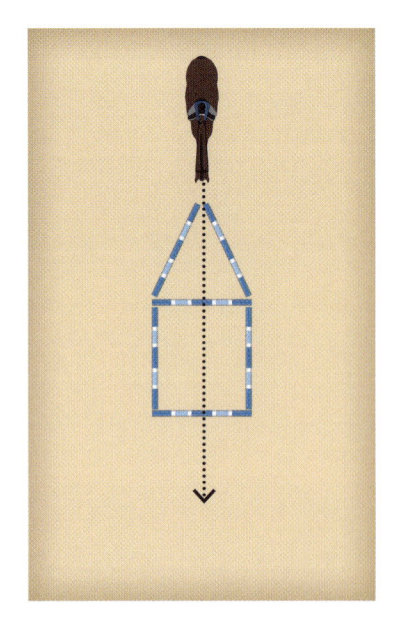

**SESSION QUESTIONS: FIRST USE**

Date of writing in journal?......................................................................................

How many times did you ride each exercise? .............................................................

How hard did you find the session?

😀   😐   😩

What did this session make you focus on most in terms of your aiding/riding?

................................................................................................................................
................................................................................................................................
................................................................................................................................
................................................................................................................................
................................................................................................................................

# Stage two

What did this session make you focus on most in terms of your horse's responses and way of going?

..................................................................................................................................
..................................................................................................................................
..................................................................................................................................
..................................................................................................................................

What would you most like to improve in your schooling for next time?

..................................................................................................................................
..................................................................................................................................
..................................................................................................................................
..................................................................................................................................

69

### SESSION QUESTIONS: FIRST USE

Date of writing in journal?..........................................................................................

How many times did you ride each exercise? ...............................................................

How hard did you find the session?

😃    😐    😩

What did this session make you focus on most in terms of your aiding/riding?

..................................................................................................................................

..................................................................................................................................

..................................................................................................................................

..................................................................................................................................

..................................................................................................................................

Stage two

# THE HOUSE
*Session two*

**CIRCLES THROUGH THE TRIANGLE**
As you did in chapter two with the Triangle layout, ride the circles through the triangle and add in transitions either side of the poles. Be aware that as there are more poles on the outside of the circle, your horse may be drawn to fall out towards the square.

**Key**
Black = trot
Red = trot or canter

> "To perform well in competition, your horse must focus fully on you, regardless of what's going on around the arena"

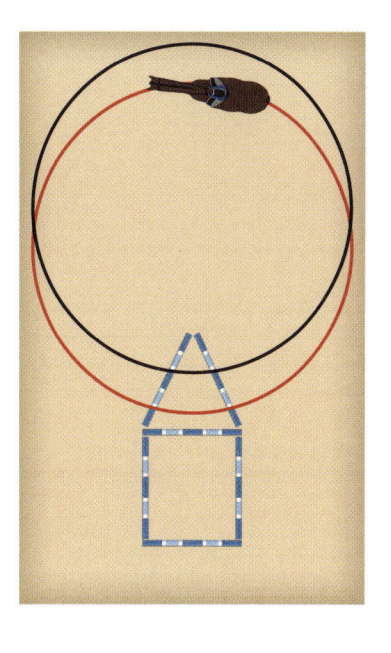

What did this session make you focus on most in terms of your horse's responses and way of going?

..................................................................................................................................
..................................................................................................................................
..................................................................................................................................
..................................................................................................................................

What would you most like to improve in your schooling for next time?

..................................................................................................................................
..................................................................................................................................
..................................................................................................................................
..................................................................................................................................

71

# THE HOUSE
## *Session three*

**DOGLEG TURNS**
In walk and trot, start on the centre line and enter over the central stripe of the square. Ride a smooth turn to go out of the side of the triangle. Ride it in both directions, so that you curve left and right.

**Next level**
To level up the exercise, ride it the other way around, so you come in through the side of the triangle and out of the centre of the square. Again, ride in both directions evenly.

Play around with the angle in which you ride your turn in terms of where you enter and exit the triangle. Find the line that is comfortable and easy for your horse, then push the angle to encourage them to open up and stretch a little more.

### SESSION QUESTIONS: FIRST USE

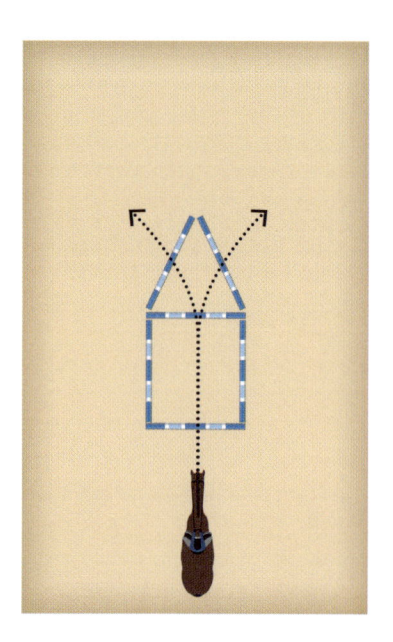

Date of writing in journal?......................................................................................

How many times did you ride each exercise?.........................................................

How hard did you find the session?

😃   😐   😩

What did this session make you focus on most in terms of your aiding/riding?

...........................................................................................................................

...........................................................................................................................

...........................................................................................................................

...........................................................................................................................

...........................................................................................................................

Stage two

**Always ride exercises evenly on both reins.**

What did this session make you focus on most in terms of your horse's responses and way of going?

..................................................................................................................................
..................................................................................................................................
..................................................................................................................................
..................................................................................................................................

What would you most like to improve in your schooling for next time?

..................................................................................................................................
..................................................................................................................................
..................................................................................................................................
..................................................................................................................................

Date ................................................Session ................................................................................

Did you find it easier or harder than the first time?...................................................................

If this has changed, why do you think it has changed?

..............................................................................................................................................................

..............................................................................................................................................................

..............................................................................................................................................................

How would you like to improve it next time?

..............................................................................................................................................................

..............................................................................................................................................................

..............................................................................................................................................................

Date ................................................Session ................................................................................

Did you find it easier or harder than the first time?...................................................................

If this has changed, why do you think it has changed?

..............................................................................................................................................................

..............................................................................................................................................................

..............................................................................................................................................................

How would you like to improve it next time?

..............................................................................................................................................................

..............................................................................................................................................................

..............................................................................................................................................................

**THINK ABOUT... WHAT HAS CHANGED | YOUR AIDS**

*Stage two*

Date .................................Session ....................................................

Did you find it easier or harder than the first time?......................................................

If this has changed, why do you think it has changed?
..................................................................................................................
..................................................................................................................
..................................................................................................................

How would you like to improve it next time?
..................................................................................................................
..................................................................................................................
..................................................................................................................

**NOTES**

..................................................................................................................
..................................................................................................................
..................................................................................................................
..................................................................................................................
..................................................................................................................
..................................................................................................................
..................................................................................................................
..................................................................................................................
..................................................................................................................
..................................................................................................................
..................................................................................................................

| YOUR HORSE'S RESPONSE | YOUR HORSE'S WAY OF GOING

# STINGRAY
*Session one*

> **SET UP**
> Start with X in the centre of the square and the tail – a tramline of poles – running either side of the centre line. Use the stride length you calculated on page five.

**CENTRE LINE IN TROT WITH TRANSITIONS**
Start by riding the centre line going in via the tail, through the centre of the square and out of the point of the triangle. Ride this in the other direction, in through the triangle and out of the tail. Then, add in halt transitions – going in both directions – halting in the tail or in the square.

Take it to the next level by riding a halt transition in the tail, rein back and proceed in trot through the rest of the exercise. Focus on maintaining straightness between both sides, using your upper leg for steering and lower leg for activity. Plan your halt in advance. It's very common to overshoot on the first attempt. If this happens, adjust your aiding and preparation to start a stride or two earlier next time.

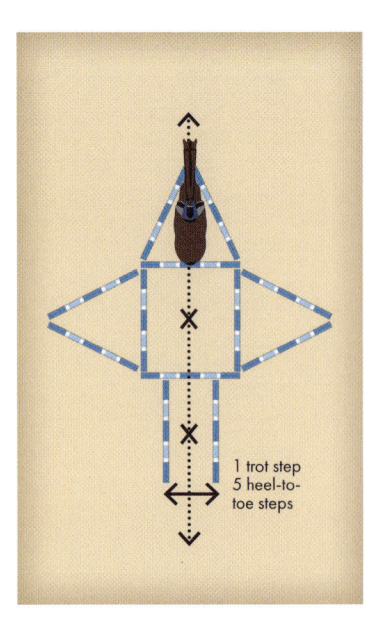

1 trot step
5 heel-to-toe steps

> **SESSION QUESTIONS: FIRST USE**

Date of writing in journal?......................................................................

How many times did you ride each exercise? ..............................................

How hard did you find the session?

😃   😐   😩

What did this session make you focus on most in terms of your aiding/riding?

..................................................................................................
..................................................................................................
..................................................................................................
..................................................................................................
..................................................................................................

Stage three

What did this session make you focus on most in terms of your horse's responses and way of going?
......................................................................................................................................
......................................................................................................................................
......................................................................................................................................
......................................................................................................................................

What would you most like to improve in your schooling for next time?
......................................................................................................................................
......................................................................................................................................
......................................................................................................................................
......................................................................................................................................

### SESSION QUESTIONS: FIRST USE

Date of writing in journal?......................................................................................

How many times did you ride each exercise? ............................................................

How hard did you find the session?

😃     😐     😩

What did this session make you focus on most in terms of your aiding/riding?

..................................................................................................................................

..................................................................................................................................

..................................................................................................................................

..................................................................................................................................

..................................................................................................................................

Stage three

# STINGRAY
*Session two*

**20M CIRCLES**
Ride 20m circles over the layout, going triangle, square, triangle. Use the stripes on the poles as a guide and ensure you cross symmetrical stripes both sides. Focus on maintaining bend and turning every stride to keep the circle a smooth, even shape. Make sure you continue to ride the circle after the poles.

**Key**
Black = walk or trot
Red = walk, trot or canter

> "It sounds obvious, but circles are symmetrical, so you must turn exactly the same amount every stride"

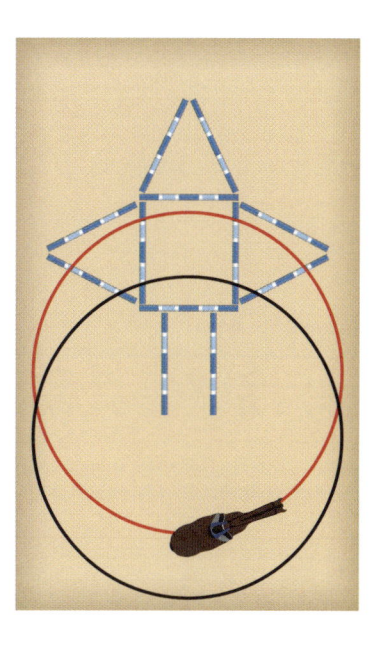

What did this session make you focus on most in terms of your horse's responses and way of going?

..................................................................................................................................
..................................................................................................................................
..................................................................................................................................
..................................................................................................................................

What would you most like to improve in your schooling for next time?

..................................................................................................................................
..................................................................................................................................
..................................................................................................................................
..................................................................................................................................

# STINGRAY
*Session three*

**FIGURE OF EIGHT**
This exercise can be ridden as two half-circles or as a continuous figure of eight. Try to keep your lines symmetrical. Riding as a full figure of eight helps improve your horse's adjustability, as you can directly compare the change of bend in both directions.

There are several common mistakes when riding this movement, such as...

- not crossing X at a right angle. When crossing the centre line, you should be parallel to the short side for at least one stride. Riders tend to either not turn far enough to end up crossing it on a diagonal, or over turn to end up with an S curve, rather than hitting it parallel
- uneven circles. Horses are one-sided and tend to fall in on one rein and out on the other. This often results in uneven circles

Use the poles as guidelines to help with the accuracy and placement of the circles. In rising trot, change your diagonal in the square when crossing the centre line.

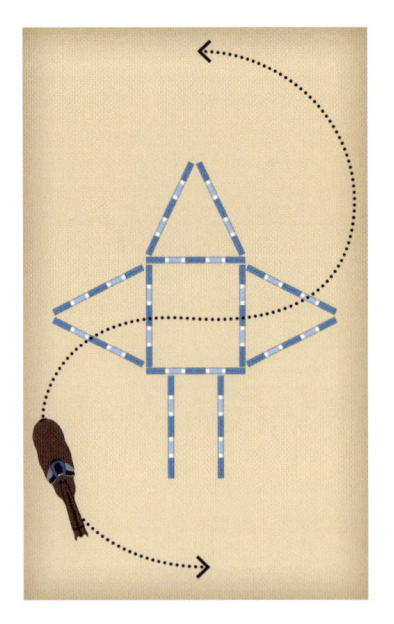

## SESSION QUESTIONS: FIRST USE

Date of writing in journal?..................................................................................

How many times did you ride each exercise? ..........................................

How hard did you find the session?

😀    😐    😩

What did this session make you focus on most in terms of your aiding/riding?

..................................................................................................................................
..................................................................................................................................
..................................................................................................................................
..................................................................................................................................
..................................................................................................................................

Stage three

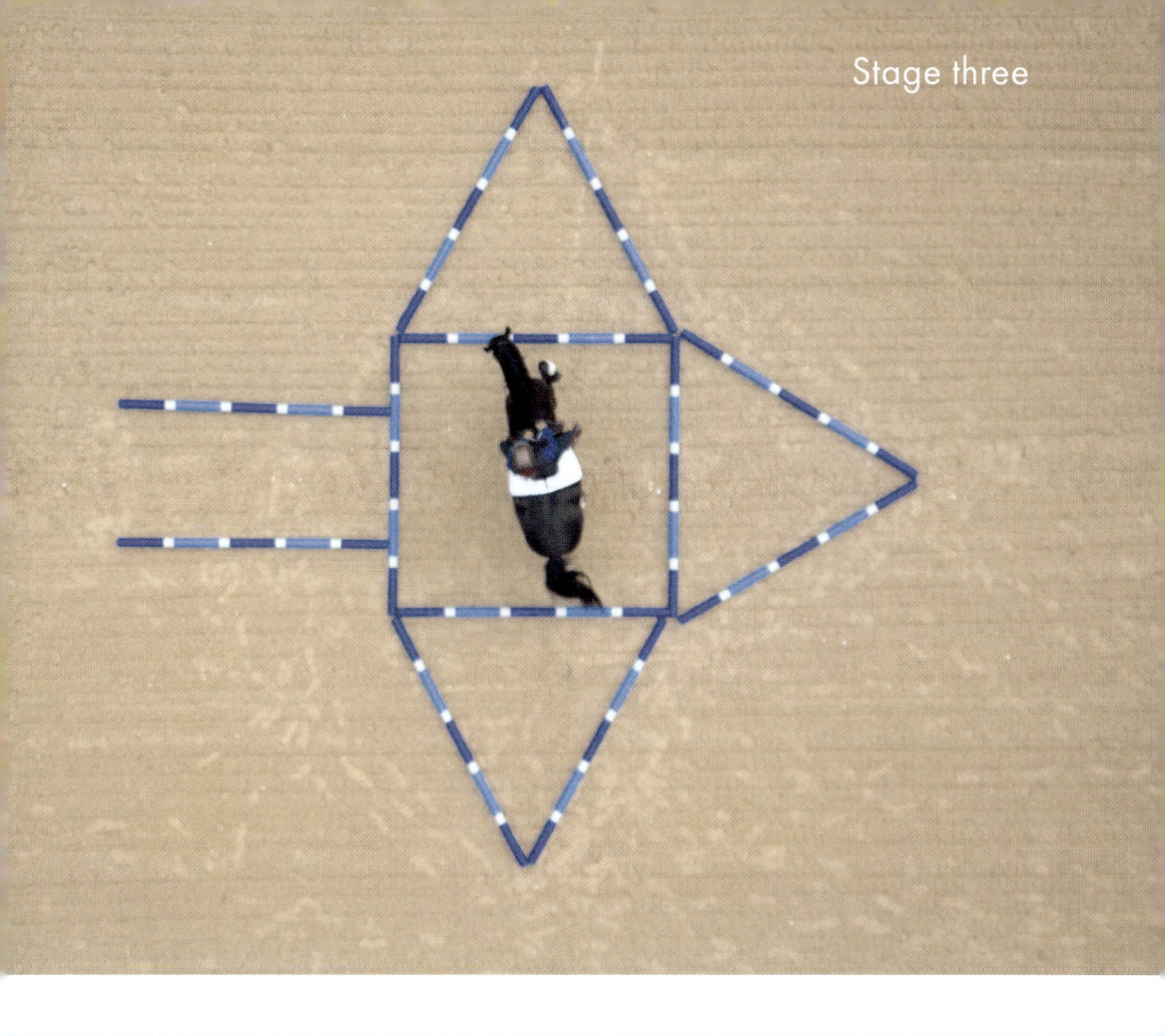

What did this session make you focus on most in terms of your horse's responses and way of going?

..................................................................................................................................
..................................................................................................................................
..................................................................................................................................
..................................................................................................................................

What would you most like to improve in your schooling for next time?

..................................................................................................................................
..................................................................................................................................
..................................................................................................................................
..................................................................................................................................

81

Date .................................................Session ..............................................................................

Did you find it easier or harder than the first time?........................................................

If this has changed, why do you think it has changed?

..............................................................................................................................................
..............................................................................................................................................
..............................................................................................................................................

How would you like to improve it next time?

..............................................................................................................................................
..............................................................................................................................................
..............................................................................................................................................

Date .................................................Session ..............................................................................

Did you find it easier or harder than the first time?........................................................

If this has changed, why do you think it has changed?

..............................................................................................................................................
..............................................................................................................................................
..............................................................................................................................................

How would you like to improve it next time?

..............................................................................................................................................
..............................................................................................................................................
..............................................................................................................................................

**THINK ABOUT... WHAT HAS CHANGED | YOUR AIDS**

# Stage three

Date .............................................. Session ..........................................................

Did you find it easier or harder than the first time?..........................................

If this has changed, why do you think it has changed?
..................................................................................................................
..................................................................................................................
..................................................................................................................

How would you like to improve it next time?
..................................................................................................................
..................................................................................................................
..................................................................................................................

## NOTES

..................................................................................................................
..................................................................................................................
..................................................................................................................
..................................................................................................................
..................................................................................................................
..................................................................................................................
..................................................................................................................
..................................................................................................................
..................................................................................................................
..................................................................................................................
..................................................................................................................

| YOUR HORSE'S RESPONSE | YOUR HORSE'S WAY OF GOING

CHAPTER FOUR

# Trial by Triangles

**BOWTIE • MIRRORED TRIANGLES • TRIAL BY TRIANGLES**

This is one of the first layouts I ever designed. I often have at least one of the stages set out at home. As the name suggests, it's purely made up of triangles, meaning it's super-versatile, with numerous options for all three paces.

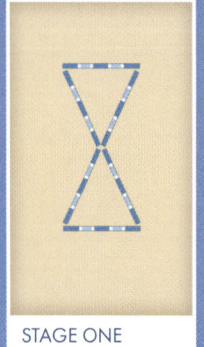

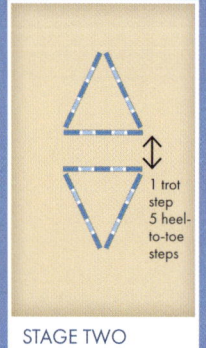

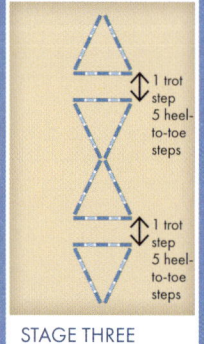

| STAGE ONE | STAGE TWO | STAGE THREE |

Stage Two: 1 trot step 5 heel-to-toe steps

Stage Three: 1 trot step 5 heel-to-toe steps (top); 1 trot step 5 heel-to-toe steps (bottom)

84

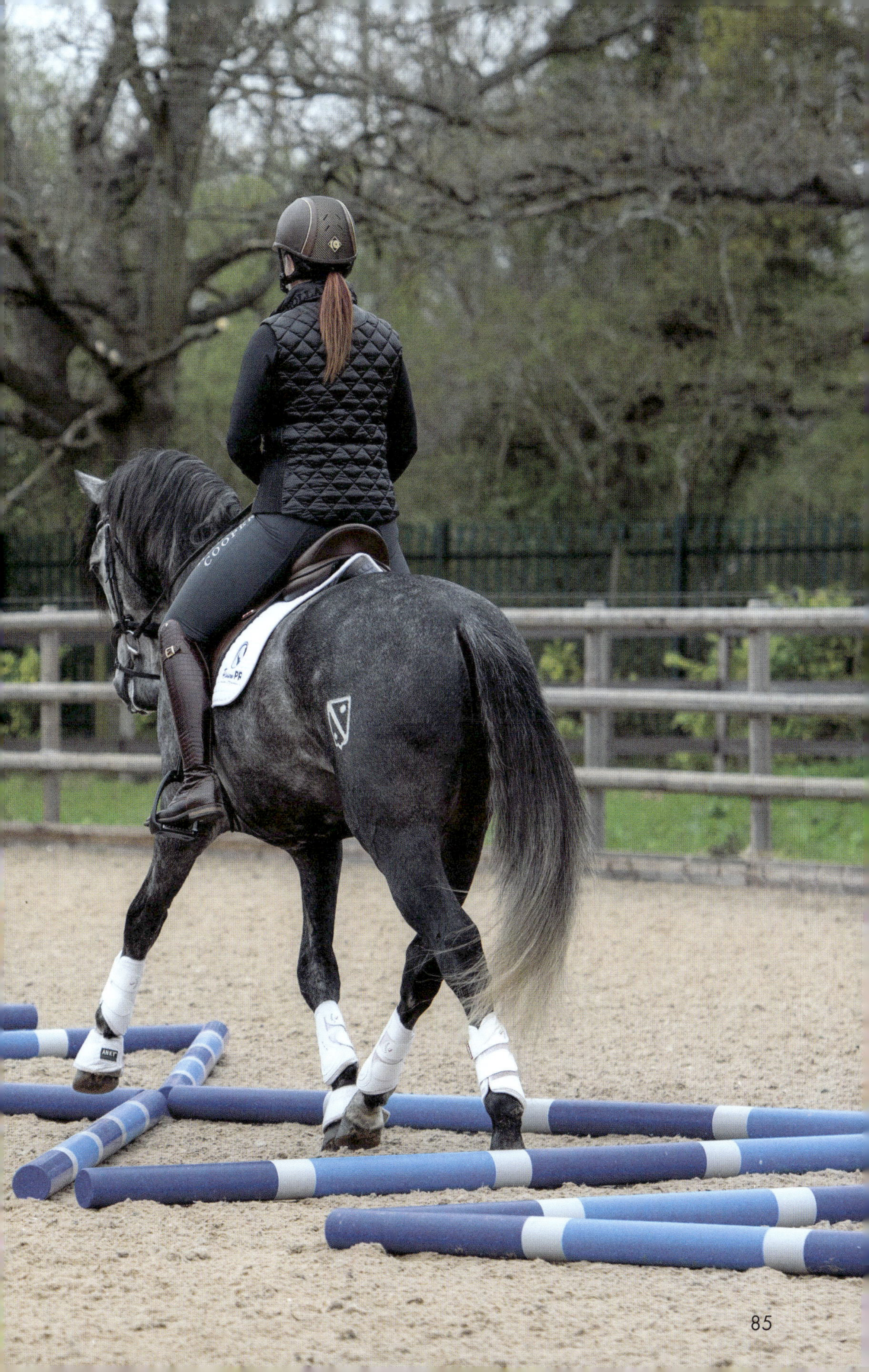

# BOW TIE
*Session one*

### SET UP
Build this layout so the point where the triangles meet is on the centre line around X, and the centre line runs straight through the triangles.

**STRAIGHT LINES**
Each triangle has two lines that can be ridden in walk, trot or canter.
**Level 1:** ride all the lines, entering over the middle of the pole at the base of the triangle and going out over a point.
**Level 2:** ride all the lines the other way around, entering over a point and out over the base.
**Level 3:** add in transitions either side of the poles.

In this exercise, focus on maintaining a straight line, before and after the poles, as well as over them. To do this, you need to plan ahead, so use the poles as a guide for your line and keep the horse upright between both legs and reins.

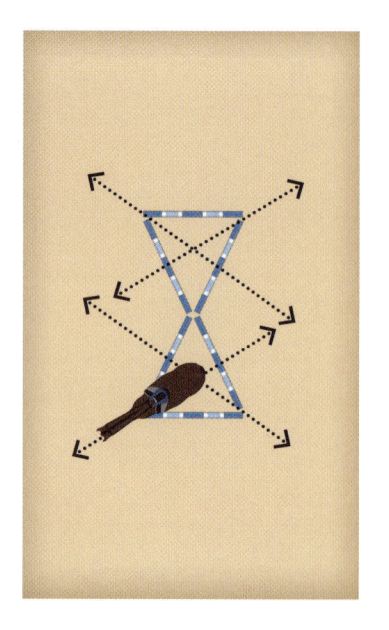

### SESSION QUESTIONS: FIRST USE

Date of writing in journal?......................................................................................

How many times did you ride each exercise? ..........................................................

How hard did you find the session?

😃   😐   😩

What did this session make you focus on most in terms of your aiding/riding?

..........................................................................................................................
..........................................................................................................................
..........................................................................................................................
..........................................................................................................................
..........................................................................................................................

86

## Stage one

> If you're struggling with straightness, you may need to lower and widen your hand position keeping your elbows bent on your sides. Focus on keeping your hips square – a crooked horse will try to push one hip forwards.

What did this session make you focus on most in terms of your horse's responses and way of going?

..................................................................................................................................
..................................................................................................................................
..................................................................................................................................
..................................................................................................................................

What would you most like to improve in your schooling for next time?

..................................................................................................................................
..................................................................................................................................
..................................................................................................................................
..................................................................................................................................

### SESSION QUESTIONS: FIRST USE

Date of writing in journal?......................................................................................................

How many times did you ride each exercise? ...................................................................

How hard did you find the session?

😀　　　😐　　　😧

What did this session make you focus on most in terms of your aiding/riding?

..............................................................................................................................................

..............................................................................................................................................

..............................................................................................................................................

..............................................................................................................................................

..............................................................................................................................................

Stage one

# BOW TIE
*Session two*

**CIRCLES THROUGH THE TRIANGLES**
You've already ridden circles through triangles in chapter two. This time, start in whatever pace you find most useful and build from there. Vary the exercise by riding circles in different paces, adding in transitions and changing which of the triangles you ride over.

People often think they must work through the paces in order but this is not true. Some horses find trot easier, others canter. I'm a firm believer in starting in your horse's easiest pace and building from there.

**Key**
Black = walk and trot
Red = walk, trot and canter

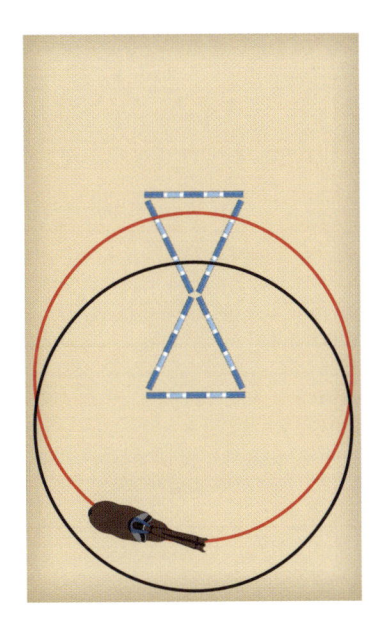

What did this session make you focus on most in terms of your horse's responses and way of going?

..............................................................................................................................
..............................................................................................................................
..............................................................................................................................
..............................................................................................................................

What would you most like to improve in your schooling for next time?

..............................................................................................................................
..............................................................................................................................
..............................................................................................................................
..............................................................................................................................

89

# BOW TIE
*Session three*

**CENTRE LINE IN TROT**
Ride straight through the layout along the centre line. The horse should place one front foot inside the triangle before the cross and the next foot inside the next triangle after the cross (red on the diagram).

To do this, the horse will have to remain totally straight and really push from behind, bending all the joints. In general, horses will try to find the easiest option, and, in this case, it's very common for them to try to step to the side of the cross (blue on the diagram).

Don't worry if this happens. Correct the straightness as you would normally and keep the upper arm and leg closed on the side they are drifting towards. It may take several attempts to be able to stay totally straight over the exercise.

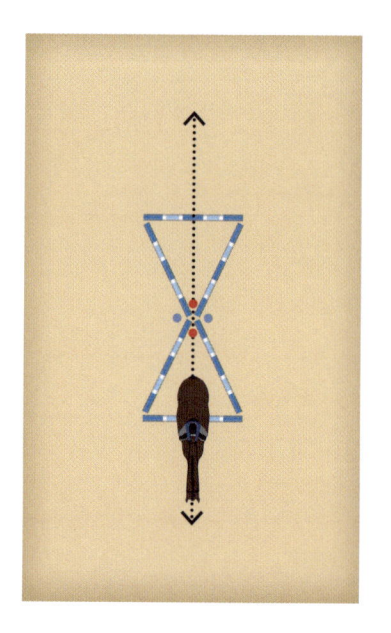

## SESSION QUESTIONS: FIRST USE

Date of writing in journal?............................................................................

How many times did you ride each exercise? ............................................

How hard did you find the session?

😃     😐     😩

What did this session make you focus on most in terms of your aiding/riding?

............................................................................................................
............................................................................................................
............................................................................................................
............................................................................................................
............................................................................................................

## Stage one

What did this session make you focus on most in terms of your horse's responses and way of going?

..................................................................................................................................
..................................................................................................................................
..................................................................................................................................
..................................................................................................................................

What would you most like to improve in your schooling for next time?

..................................................................................................................................
..................................................................................................................................
..................................................................................................................................
..................................................................................................................................

Date ............................................Session ........................................................................

Did you find it easier or harder than the first time?................................................................

If this has changed, why do you think it has changed?

................................................................................................................................

................................................................................................................................

................................................................................................................................

How would you like to improve it next time?

................................................................................................................................

................................................................................................................................

................................................................................................................................

Date ............................................Session ........................................................................

Did you find it easier or harder than the first time?................................................................

If this has changed, why do you think it has changed?

................................................................................................................................

................................................................................................................................

................................................................................................................................

How would you like to improve it next time?

................................................................................................................................

................................................................................................................................

................................................................................................................................

**THINK ABOUT... WHAT HAS CHANGED | YOUR AIDS**

*Stage one*

Date ..............................................Session ................................................................

Did you find it easier or harder than the first time?.........................................................

If this has changed, why do you think it has changed?
..............................................................................................................................
..............................................................................................................................
..............................................................................................................................

How would you like to improve it next time?
..............................................................................................................................
..............................................................................................................................
..............................................................................................................................

**NOTES**

..............................................................................................................................
..............................................................................................................................
..............................................................................................................................
..............................................................................................................................
..............................................................................................................................
..............................................................................................................................
..............................................................................................................................
..............................................................................................................................
..............................................................................................................................
..............................................................................................................................
..............................................................................................................................

| YOUR HORSE'S RESPONSE | YOUR HORSE'S WAY OF GOING

# MIRRORED TRIANGLES

*Session one*

### SET UP
Position your poles so that the points face A and C and the gap runs from E–B.

### TRANSITIONS
Use the gap to work on the placement and accuracy of your transitions.
- ride single transitions centred in the gap; for example, a canter strike off over the centre line or a trot–halt–trot transition (black cross)
- ride sequence transitions and centre the middle pace between the gap, with transitions either side. For example, trot–walk–trot, or canter–trot–canter (blue crosses)

1 trot step
5 heel-to-toe steps

### SESSION QUESTIONS: FIRST USE

Date of writing in journal?..................................................................

How many times did you ride each exercise? ...............................................

How hard did you find the session?

😄   😐   😩

What did this session make you focus on most in terms of your aiding/riding?

..................................................................................................

..................................................................................................

..................................................................................................

..................................................................................................

..................................................................................................

Stage two

What did this session make you focus on most in terms of your horse's responses and way of going?
..................................................................................................................................
..................................................................................................................................
..................................................................................................................................
..................................................................................................................................

What would you most like to improve in your schooling for next time?
..................................................................................................................................
..................................................................................................................................
..................................................................................................................................
..................................................................................................................................

### SESSION QUESTIONS: FIRST USE

Date of writing in journal?..................................................................................

How many times did you ride each exercise? ............................................

How hard did you find the session?

😃    😐    😩

What did this session make you focus on most in terms of your aiding/riding?

..................................................................................................................

..................................................................................................................

..................................................................................................................

..................................................................................................................

..................................................................................................................

Stage two

# MIRRORED TRIANGLES
*Session two*

**CENTRE LINE IN TROT**
Focus on riding balanced turns onto and off the centre line either side of the poles. As with the earlier exercises, you may need to widen and lower your hand position initially to help with straightness.

"Centre lines can never be practised too much! Every test has at least two and so many movements are performed from centre line turns"

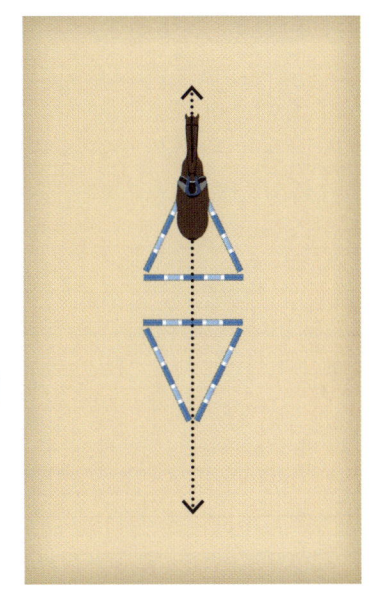

What did this session make you focus on most in terms of your horse's responses and way of going?

..........................................................................................................................................
..........................................................................................................................................
..........................................................................................................................................
..........................................................................................................................................

What would you most like to improve in your schooling for next time?

..........................................................................................................................................
..........................................................................................................................................
..........................................................................................................................................
..........................................................................................................................................

# MIRRORED TRIANGLES
*Session three*

**10M LOOP IN TROT**
From the corner of the arena, ride a smooth, continuous loop that touches the centre line at the gap in the poles. Your loop should be symmetrical and cross the equivalent stripe on the poles on both sides of the layout. This is tricky to achieve, so may take several attempts.

Focus on making many small adjustments to ride the line and make sure you ride it on both reins.

> "If the loop is 10m, this means you should be on the centre line for at least one stride"

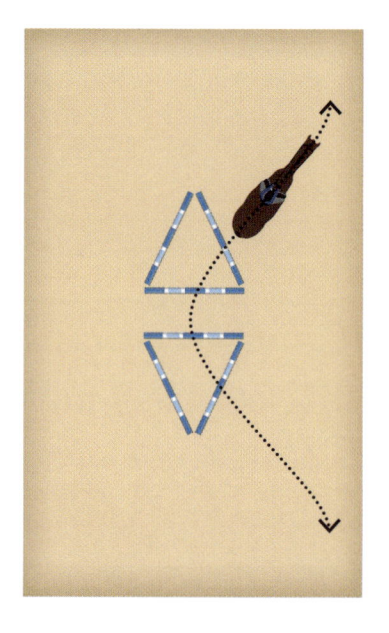

## SESSION QUESTIONS: FIRST USE

Date of writing in journal?..................................................................................

How many times did you ride each exercise? ...................................................

How hard did you find the session?

😃     😐     😩

What did this session make you focus on most in terms of your aiding/riding?

...................................................................................................................
...................................................................................................................
...................................................................................................................
...................................................................................................................
...................................................................................................................

98

Stage two

What did this session make you focus on most in terms of your horse's responses and way of going?

..............................................................................................................................................
..............................................................................................................................................
..............................................................................................................................................
..............................................................................................................................................

What would you most like to improve in your schooling for next time?

..............................................................................................................................................
..............................................................................................................................................
..............................................................................................................................................
..............................................................................................................................................

Date ..................................................Session ............................................................................

Did you find it easier or harder than the first time?...............................................................

If this has changed, why do you think it has changed?

..................................................................................................................................................

..................................................................................................................................................

..................................................................................................................................................

How would you like to improve it next time?

..................................................................................................................................................

..................................................................................................................................................

..................................................................................................................................................


Date ..................................................Session ............................................................................

Did you find it easier or harder than the first time?...............................................................

If this has changed, why do you think it has changed?

..................................................................................................................................................

..................................................................................................................................................

..................................................................................................................................................

How would you like to improve it next time?

..................................................................................................................................................

..................................................................................................................................................

..................................................................................................................................................

**THINK ABOUT... WHAT HAS CHANGED | YOUR AIDS**

## Stage two

Date .................................................Session ..............................................................................

Did you find it easier or harder than the first time?......................................................

If this has changed, why do you think it has changed?
..................................................................................................................................
..................................................................................................................................
..................................................................................................................................

How would you like to improve it next time?
..................................................................................................................................
..................................................................................................................................
..................................................................................................................................

**NOTES**

..........................................................................................................................................
..........................................................................................................................................
..........................................................................................................................................
..........................................................................................................................................
..........................................................................................................................................
..........................................................................................................................................
..........................................................................................................................................
..........................................................................................................................................
..........................................................................................................................................
..........................................................................................................................................
..........................................................................................................................................

| YOUR HORSE'S RESPONSE | YOUR HORSE'S WAY OF GOING

# TRIAL BY TRIANGLES
*Session one*

> **SET UP**
> Position your layout along the centre line so each end points to A and C.

**CENTRE LINE IN TROT**
You have already ridden centre lines in the first two stages of this chapter and, as with the Bow Tie layout, you want the horse to remain totally straight and only step within the triangles over the central section of the layout.

To do this, your horse must remain totally upright and balanced to push from behind and step over all the poles.

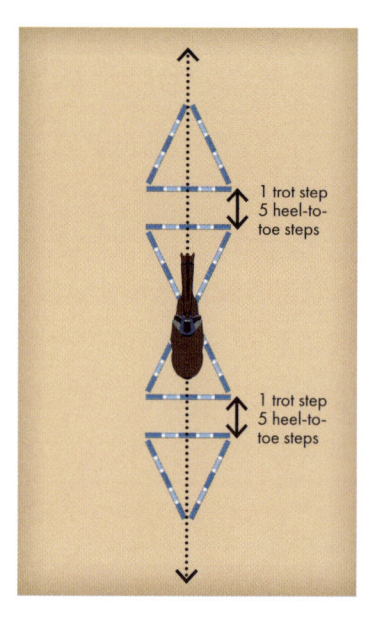

1 trot step
5 heel-to-toe steps

1 trot step
5 heel-to-toe steps

---

**SESSION QUESTIONS: FIRST USE**

Date of writing in journal?..........................................................................

How many times did you ride each exercise? .........................................

How hard did you find the session?

😃    😐    😩

What did this session make you focus on most in terms of your aiding/riding?

..................................................................................................................
..................................................................................................................
..................................................................................................................
..................................................................................................................
..................................................................................................................

102

Stage three

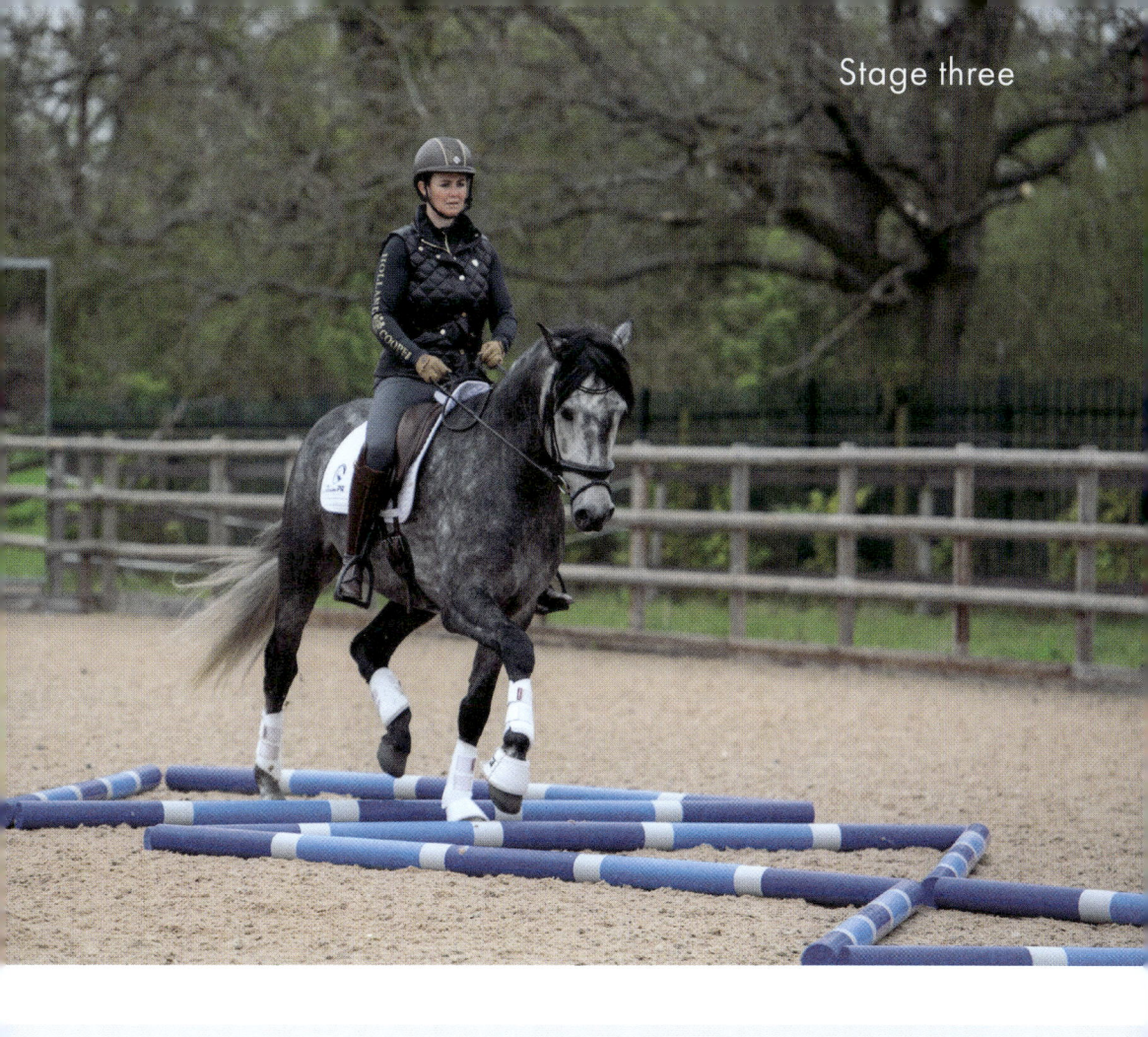

What did this session make you focus on most in terms of your horse's responses and way of going?
..................................................................................................................................
..................................................................................................................................
..................................................................................................................................
..................................................................................................................................

What would you most like to improve in your schooling for next time?
..................................................................................................................................
..................................................................................................................................
..................................................................................................................................
..................................................................................................................................

### SESSION QUESTIONS: FIRST USE

Date of writing in journal?..............................................................................

How many times did you ride each exercise? ..............................................

How hard did you find the session?

😀  😐  😩

What did this session make you focus on most in terms of your aiding/riding?

....................................................................................................................
....................................................................................................................
....................................................................................................................
....................................................................................................................
....................................................................................................................

104

Stage three

# TRIAL BY TRIANGLES
*Session two*

**10M LOOP IN TROT**
As with the loop over the Mirrored Triangles layout, your line should be smooth, symmetrical and on a continuous curve. Use the stripes on the poles to check for symmetry. You should touch the centre line over the cross in the centre.

Focus on planning ahead with your line and aiding to give your horse plenty of warning as to where you want them to go.

## "Make sure you look up towards A or C as you aim for the centre line"

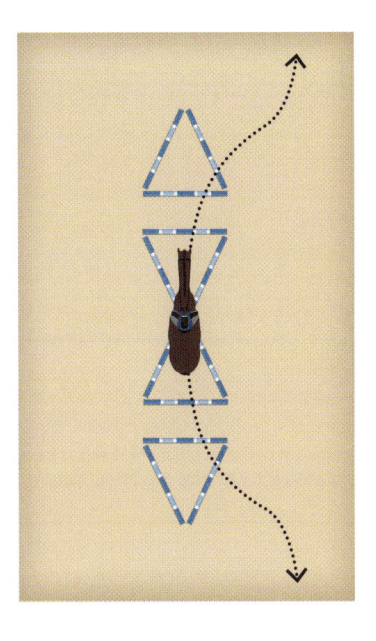

What did this session make you focus on most in terms of your horse's responses and way of going?

..............................................................................................................................
..............................................................................................................................
..............................................................................................................................
..............................................................................................................................

What would you most like to improve in your schooling for next time?

..............................................................................................................................
..............................................................................................................................
..............................................................................................................................
..............................................................................................................................

# TRIAL BY TRIANGLES
*Session three*

**DOGLEG AND DOUBLE DOGLEG**
For the dogleg (blue line), start by riding straight along the centre line in over the point of the first pole. Remain straight through the centre of the exercise and ride a smooth, curved line to exit the layout over the side of the triangle. Ride this turning in both directions.

To level up the exercise ride in reverse, in over the side of the triangle, straight though the middle and out through the point on the centre line. Once again, ride the turn in both directions.

For the double dogleg (black line), from the corner of the arena, ride a diagonal line that enters over the side of the first triangle, goes straight over the centre of the layout and out over the opposite side of the last triangle. Ride this on both reins.

Focus on giving your horse warning of the line you want him to take. Make sure you remain upright, with your shoulders level as you ride the turns, as this will help your horse remain upright and level as well.

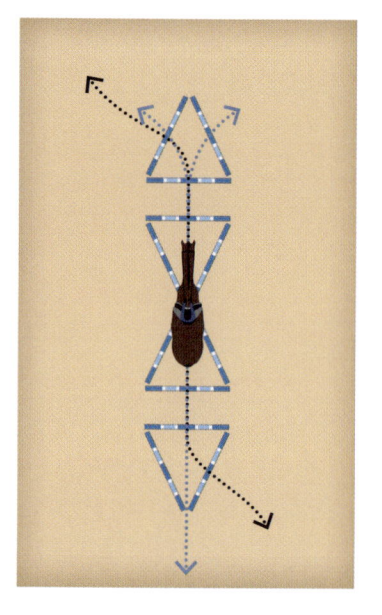

## SESSION QUESTIONS: FIRST USE

Date of writing in journal?..............................................................................

How many times did you ride each exercise? .............................................

How hard did you find the session?

😃    😐    😩

What did this session make you focus on most in terms of your aiding/riding?

..................................................................................................................

..................................................................................................................

..................................................................................................................

..................................................................................................................

Stage three

What did this session make you focus on most in terms of your horse's responses and way of going?

..................................................................................................................................................
..................................................................................................................................................
..................................................................................................................................................
..................................................................................................................................................

What would you most like to improve in your schooling for next time?

..................................................................................................................................................
..................................................................................................................................................
..................................................................................................................................................
..................................................................................................................................................

Date ................................................Session .................................................................

Did you find it easier or harder than the first time?..................................................

If this has changed, why do you think it has changed?

....................................................................................................................................

....................................................................................................................................

....................................................................................................................................

How would you like to improve it next time?

....................................................................................................................................

....................................................................................................................................

....................................................................................................................................


Date ................................................Session .................................................................

Did you find it easier or harder than the first time?..................................................

If this has changed, why do you think it has changed?

....................................................................................................................................

....................................................................................................................................

....................................................................................................................................

How would you like to improve it next time?

....................................................................................................................................

....................................................................................................................................

....................................................................................................................................

**THINK ABOUT...** WHAT HAS CHANGED | YOUR AIDS

# Stage three

Date ................................................Session ................................................................

Did you find it easier or harder than the first time?................................................

If this has changed, why do you think it has changed?

................................................................................................................................

................................................................................................................................

................................................................................................................................

How would you like to improve it next time?

................................................................................................................................

................................................................................................................................

................................................................................................................................

## NOTES

................................................................................................................................

................................................................................................................................

................................................................................................................................

................................................................................................................................

................................................................................................................................

................................................................................................................................

................................................................................................................................

................................................................................................................................

................................................................................................................................

................................................................................................................................

| YOUR HORSE'S RESPONSE | YOUR HORSE'S WAY OF GOING

CHAPTER FIVE

# Spider Web

## ZIGZAG • BUNTING • SPIDER WEB

All poles help to increase engagement of the hind leg and create more lift in the pace. Using this layout, you will often be crossing the poles at an angle in the trot work. Horses' vision is different from ours, as they find it hard to make out details at close range. In effect, this means that when crossing angled poles, they find it harder to judge the distances and therefore tend to put in more effort, which results in more lift within the pace.

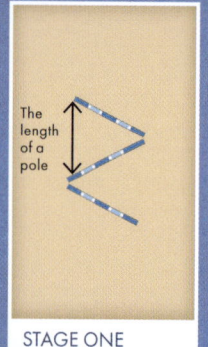

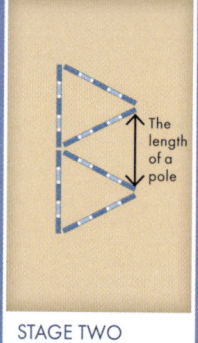

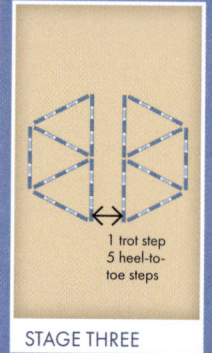

The length of a pole

STAGE ONE

The length of a pole

STAGE TWO

1 trot step
5 heel-to-toe steps

STAGE THREE

110

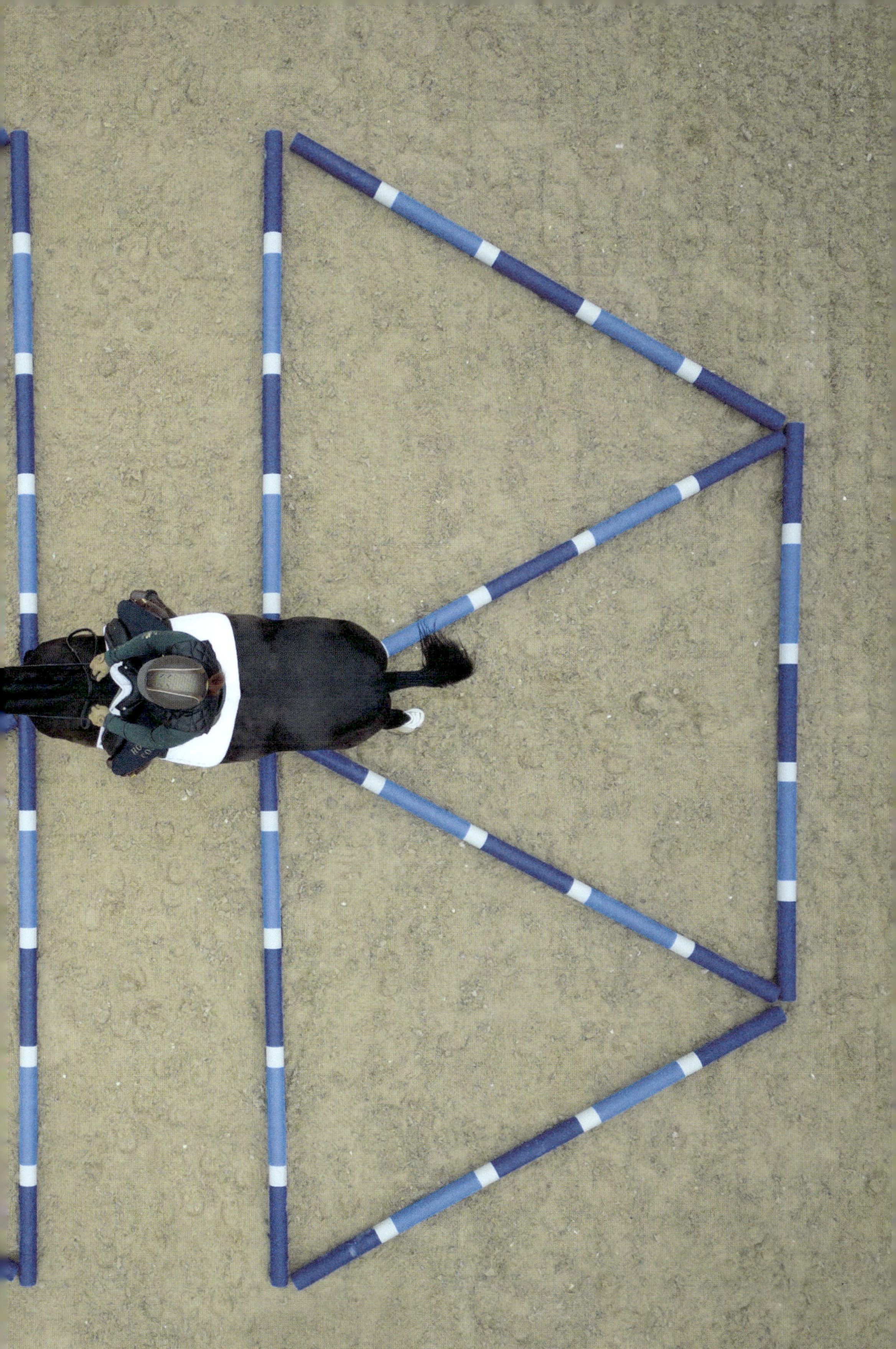

# ZIGZAG
*Session one*

> **SET UP**
> You want to position the zigzag so that it runs along the centre or the three-quarter line of the arena, with the points facing the long sides. The gap at the widest part of the zigzag should be one pole's length.

**STRAIGHT LINES OVER THE MIDDLE OF THE POLES**
Ride your horse straight over the centre of the poles. You can do this in walk, trot or canter. Ride single changes of rein across the diagonals (black), or a continuous line, circling around the poles (blue).

To level up, add in transitions so you cross the poles in different paces. Focus on keeping the same balance and line before and after the poles.

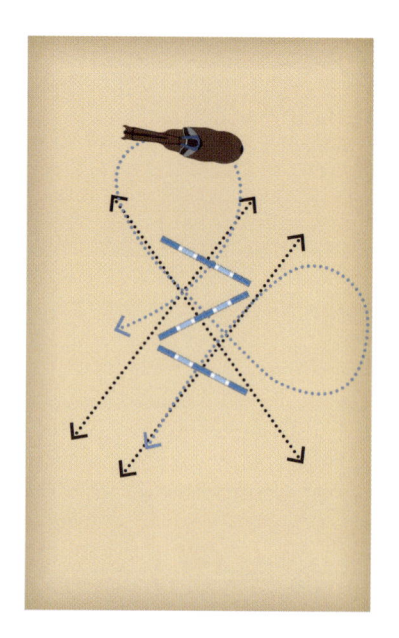

**SESSION QUESTIONS: FIRST USE**

Date of writing in journal? ....................................................................

How many times did you ride each exercise? ....................................................................

How hard did you find the session?

😃    😐    😩

What did this session make you focus on most in terms of your aiding/riding?

....................................................................
....................................................................
....................................................................
....................................................................
....................................................................

Stage one

What did this session make you focus on most in terms of your horse's responses and way of going?
..................................................................................................................................................
..................................................................................................................................................
..................................................................................................................................................
..................................................................................................................................................

What would you most like to improve in your schooling for next time?
..................................................................................................................................................
..................................................................................................................................................
..................................................................................................................................................
..................................................................................................................................................

**SESSION QUESTIONS: FIRST USE**

Date of writing in journal?..............................................................................

How many times did you ride each exercise? .................................................

How hard did you find the session?

😃     😐     😩

What did this session make you focus on most in terms of your aiding/riding?

................................................................................................................

................................................................................................................

................................................................................................................

................................................................................................................

................................................................................................................

Stage one

# ZIGZAG
*Session two*

**STRAIGHT LINES OVER THE POINTS OF THE POLES**
With these exercises, instead of going over the middle of the poles, you will ride over the point where two poles come together. You can ride these lines in walk, trot or canter, but if your horse is unsure of going over the point, start off in walk.
**Level 1:** ride over a point that's facing away from you
**Level 2:** ride over a point that's facing towards you

The point facing away is more inviting for your horse and will be easier for you to keep him straight. When riding over the point that's facing towards you, focus on maintaining straightness between both legs and reins.

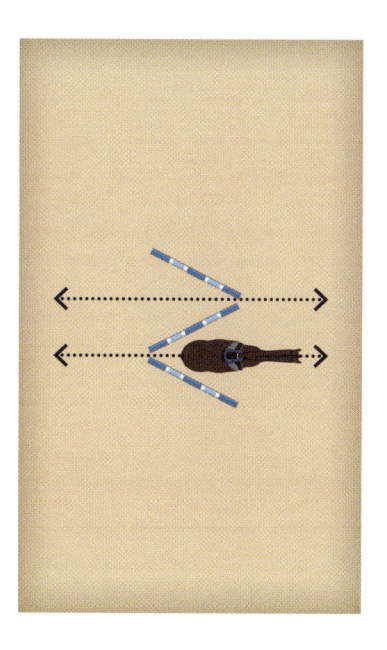

What did this session make you focus on most in terms of your horse's responses and way of going?

..................................................................................................................................
..................................................................................................................................
..................................................................................................................................
..................................................................................................................................

What would you most like to improve in your schooling for next time?

..................................................................................................................................
..................................................................................................................................
..................................................................................................................................
..................................................................................................................................

# ZIGZAG
*Session three*

**STRAIGHT LINES ALONG THE ZIGZAG**
In walk, ride a straight line off the centre of the zigzag. When in trot, make sure your line is straight through the very centre of the zigzag. Crossing the poles at an angle rather than straight will encourage the horse to really bend his joints and produce more lift in the pace. Use the stripes on the poles to help remain straight. Veering off your line will change the distance, making it hard for your horse to find his stride.

**Key**
Blue = walk
Black = trot

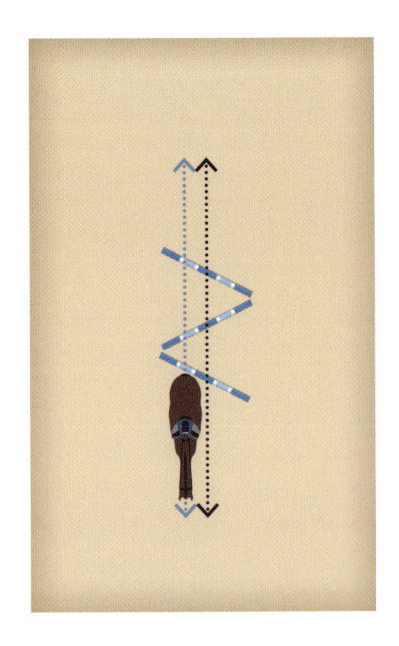

## SESSION QUESTIONS: FIRST USE

Date of writing in journal?..........................................................

How many times did you ride each exercise? ..........................

How hard did you find the session?

😀    😐    😫

What did this session make you focus on most in terms of your aiding/riding?

..........................................................................................................
..........................................................................................................
..........................................................................................................
..........................................................................................................
..........................................................................................................

Stage one

What did this session make you focus on most in terms of your horse's responses and way of going?

..................................................................................................................................
..................................................................................................................................
..................................................................................................................................
..................................................................................................................................

What would you most like to improve in your schooling for next time?

..................................................................................................................................
..................................................................................................................................
..................................................................................................................................
..................................................................................................................................

Date .............................................Session ........................................................................

Did you find it easier or harder than the first time?.........................................................

If this has changed, why do you think it has changed?

................................................................................................................................
................................................................................................................................
................................................................................................................................

How would you like to improve it next time?

................................................................................................................................
................................................................................................................................
................................................................................................................................


Date .............................................Session ........................................................................

Did you find it easier or harder than the first time?.........................................................

If this has changed, why do you think it has changed?

................................................................................................................................
................................................................................................................................
................................................................................................................................

How would you like to improve it next time?

................................................................................................................................
................................................................................................................................
................................................................................................................................

**THINK ABOUT... WHAT HAS CHANGED | YOUR AIDS**

## Stage one

Date .................................... Session ....................................................

Did you find it easier or harder than the first time? ...............................................

If this has changed, why do you think it has changed?
..................................................................................................
..................................................................................................
..................................................................................................

How would you like to improve it next time?
..................................................................................................
..................................................................................................
..................................................................................................

**NOTES**

..................................................................................................
..................................................................................................
..................................................................................................
..................................................................................................
..................................................................................................
..................................................................................................
..................................................................................................
..................................................................................................
..................................................................................................
..................................................................................................
..................................................................................................
..................................................................................................

| YOUR HORSE'S RESPONSE | YOUR HORSE'S WAY OF GOING

# BUNTING
*Session one*

> **SET UP**
> This layout can be set up on the centre or three-quarter line of the arena so the points face towards the long side.

**STRAIGHT LINES**
As in chapters two and four, straight lines can be ridden through the triangles in walk, trot and canter. The location of the triangles in relation to each other makes the straight lines in this layout a little more challenging, as the horse may be distracted by the other poles.

**Level 1:** black, base to point
**Level 2:** black, point to base
**Level 3:** blue, base to point
**Level 4:** blue, point to base
**Level 5:** red, base to point
**Level 6:** red, point to base

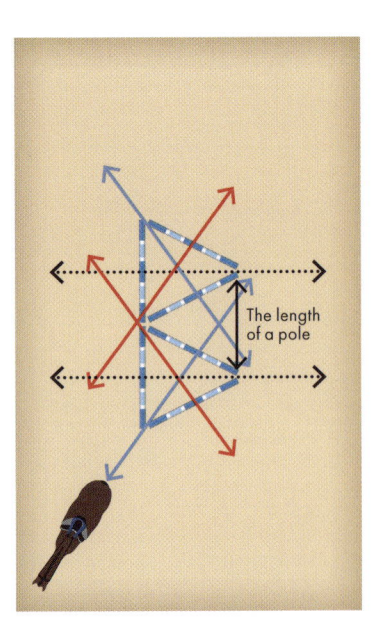

## SESSION QUESTIONS: FIRST USE

Date of writing in journal?..............................................................

How many times did you ride each exercise? ..............................

How hard did you find the session?

😃    😐    😩

What did this session make you focus on most in terms of your aiding/riding?

..........................................................................................................
..........................................................................................................
..........................................................................................................
..........................................................................................................
..........................................................................................................

Stage two

What did this session make you focus on most in terms of your horse's responses and way of going?

..................................................................................................................................
..................................................................................................................................
..................................................................................................................................
..................................................................................................................................

What would you most like to improve in your schooling for next time?

..................................................................................................................................
..................................................................................................................................
..................................................................................................................................
..................................................................................................................................

### SESSION QUESTIONS: FIRST USE

Date of writing in journal?......................................................................................

How many times did you ride each exercise? .............................................................

How hard did you find the session?

😃   😐   😩

What did this session make you focus on most in terms of your aiding/riding?

..............................................................................................................................
..............................................................................................................................
..............................................................................................................................
..............................................................................................................................
..............................................................................................................................

Stage two

# BUNTING
*Session two*

**CIRCLES OVER TRIANGLES**
You'll have ridden circles over triangles in chapters two and four, but with this layout, the poles are in a different sector of the circle. Focus on riding an accurate 20m circle, making sure you keep turning before and after the poles. It sounds obvious but when the poles are in a different place, it can almost act as an optical illusion. You can ride this exercise in walk, trot and canter.

> "Plan four points of accuracy on your circle so you know where you are aiming before and after the poles."

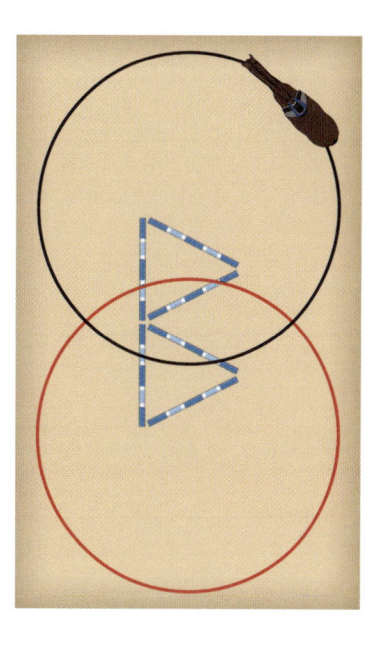

What did this session make you focus on most in terms of your horse's responses and way of going?

..................................................................................................................................
..................................................................................................................................
..................................................................................................................................
..................................................................................................................................

What would you most like to improve in your schooling for next time?

..................................................................................................................................
..................................................................................................................................
..................................................................................................................................
..................................................................................................................................

123

# BUNTING
*Session three*

**STRAIGHT LINE ALONG THE CENTRE**
As with exercise three in the Zigzag, you can ride in walk off centre, however the main focus of this exercise is trot. There are now four angled poles to trot over. In order to trot over all four poles correctly, the horse must remain totally straight and really be pushing from behind to create enough lift to clear all the poles.

This is quite a hard exercise, so don't worry if it takes several goes. The horse may need to gain confidence to be able to relax enough and have the power to do this. If you are struggling to achieve sufficient push or power in the trot to go over the poles easily, try cantering around the arena. You can even turn onto the line in canter and ask for a trot transition just before the poles. Many horses will have a naturally more powerful trot directly after the canter.

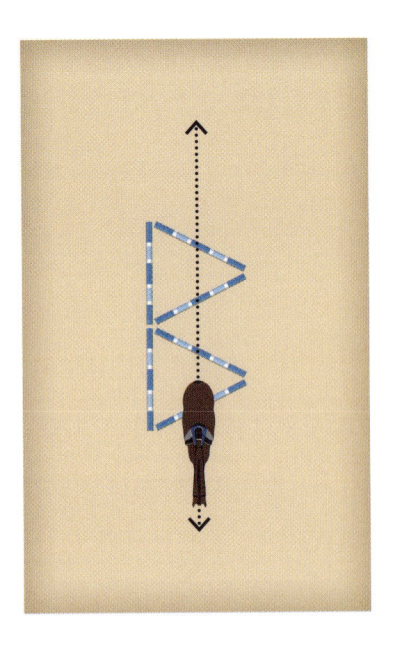

## SESSION QUESTIONS: FIRST USE

Date of writing in journal?..................................................

How many times did you ride each exercise? ..........................

How hard did you find the session?

😀　　😐　　😩

What did this session make you focus on most in terms of your aiding/riding?

..................................................................................
..................................................................................
..................................................................................
..................................................................................

*Stage two*

What did this session make you focus on most in terms of your horse's responses and way of going?

.................................................................................................................................................
.................................................................................................................................................
.................................................................................................................................................
.................................................................................................................................................

What would you most like to improve in your schooling for next time?

.................................................................................................................................................
.................................................................................................................................................
.................................................................................................................................................
.................................................................................................................................................

Date .................................................Session .................................................................................

Did you find it easier or harder than the first time?.............................................................

If this has changed, why do you think it has changed?

..............................................................................................................................................
..............................................................................................................................................
..............................................................................................................................................

How would you like to improve it next time?

..............................................................................................................................................
..............................................................................................................................................
..............................................................................................................................................

Date .................................................Session .................................................................................

Did you find it easier or harder than the first time?.............................................................

If this has changed, why do you think it has changed?

..............................................................................................................................................
..............................................................................................................................................
..............................................................................................................................................

How would you like to improve it next time?

..............................................................................................................................................
..............................................................................................................................................
..............................................................................................................................................

**THINK ABOUT...** WHAT HAS CHANGED | YOUR AIDS

## Stage two

Date .................................................Session ..........................................................................

Did you find it easier or harder than the first time?..............................................................

If this has changed, why do you think it has changed?
................................................................................................................................................
................................................................................................................................................

How would you like to improve it next time?
................................................................................................................................................
................................................................................................................................................
................................................................................................................................................

**NOTES**

................................................................................................................................................
................................................................................................................................................
................................................................................................................................................
................................................................................................................................................
................................................................................................................................................
................................................................................................................................................
................................................................................................................................................
................................................................................................................................................
................................................................................................................................................
................................................................................................................................................
................................................................................................................................................

| YOUR HORSE'S RESPONSE | YOUR HORSE'S WAY OF GOING

# SPIDER WEB
*Session one*

> **SET UP**
> Build a tramline with the poles evenly placed either side of the centre line, then create your triangles.

**STRAIGHT LINES**
Ride straight lines through the gap between the poles with transitions in the centre (black cross). Try trot to canter or a halt transition.
   Next ride transitions either side of the gap (blue crosses). Try canter–trot–canter or walk–trot–walk.
   Make this exercise work for the level you are training at with your horse. Anything that needs to be performed on a straight line can be ridden through this gap. I had fun riding my tempi changes!

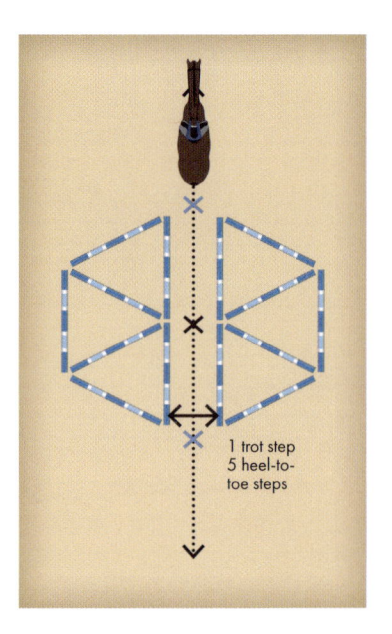

1 trot step
5 heel-to-toe steps

> **SESSION QUESTIONS: FIRST USE**

Date of writing in journal?..................................................................................

How many times did you ride each exercise? ......................................................

How hard did you find the session?

😃   😐   😰

What did this session make you focus on most in terms of your aiding/riding?

................................................................................................................
................................................................................................................
................................................................................................................
................................................................................................................
................................................................................................................

## Stage three

What did this session make you focus on most in terms of your horse's responses and way of going?

..................................................................................................................................
..................................................................................................................................
..................................................................................................................................
..................................................................................................................................

What would you most like to improve in your schooling for next time?

..................................................................................................................................
..................................................................................................................................
..................................................................................................................................
..................................................................................................................................

> If your horse is unsure about this line, take your time, allow him to go slowly and offer lots of praise when he tries, even if it's not yet perfect.

### SESSION QUESTIONS: FIRST USE

Date of writing in journal?......................................................................................

How many times did you ride each exercise? ...........................................................

How hard did you find the session?

😀    😐    😩

What did this session make you focus on most in terms of your aiding/riding?

............................................................................................................................
............................................................................................................................
............................................................................................................................
............................................................................................................................
............................................................................................................................

Stage three

# SPIDER WEB
*Session two*

**STRAIGHT LINES ACROSS THE WEB IN TROT**
**Level 1:** ride straight through the end triangles (blue). Although riding in through a point is usually harder, you should be well practised at this by now. However, now there are lots of poles to one side to distract the horse. Ride the line at both ends and use all the different ways you can turn before and after the poles, such as...
- turn left, turn left
- turn left, turn right
- turn right, turn right
- turn right, turn left

**Level 2:** ride straight through the middle triangles (black). Although entering through a base is usually easier, the central section with all the poles coming together is a lot for your horse to look at. Focus on straightness because when things are difficult, your horse may try to go crooked, but when it goes right, he will really lift and push as he navigates this exercise.

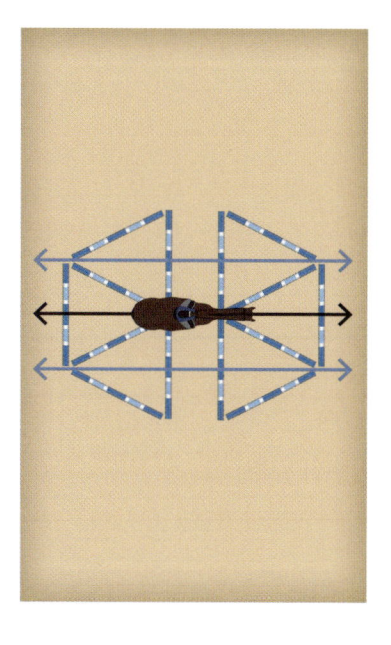

What did this session make you focus on most in terms of your horse's responses and way of going?

..................................................................................................................................................
..................................................................................................................................................
..................................................................................................................................................
..................................................................................................................................................

What would you most like to improve in your schooling for next time?

..................................................................................................................................................
..................................................................................................................................................
..................................................................................................................................................
..................................................................................................................................................

# SPIDER WEB
*Session three*

**STRAIGHT LINES THROUGH THE DIAMOND**
You can ride this exercise in walk, trot or canter. Focus on the line and the turns before and after. In both trot and canter, stay sitting up and keep the horse balanced. Do not fold in canter, because you want the horse to sit and push rather than lengthen and pull.

*"Canter poles often get horses excited; if this happens, alternate working in trot and canter over the poles"*

### SESSION QUESTIONS: FIRST USE

Date of writing in journal?..................................................................................

How many times did you ride each exercise? ............................................

How hard did you find the session?

😀     😐     😩

What did this session make you focus on most in terms of your aiding/riding?

..................................................................................................................

..................................................................................................................

..................................................................................................................

..................................................................................................................

Stage three

What did this session make you focus on most in terms of your horse's responses and way of going?
............................................................................................
............................................................................................
............................................................................................
............................................................................................

What would you most like to improve in your schooling for next time?
............................................................................................
............................................................................................
............................................................................................
............................................................................................

Date .................................................Session ....................................................

Did you find it easier or harder than the first time?........................................................

If this has changed, why do you think it has changed?

..............................................................................................................................

..............................................................................................................................

..............................................................................................................................

How would you like to improve it next time?

..............................................................................................................................

..............................................................................................................................

..............................................................................................................................


Date .................................................Session ....................................................

Did you find it easier or harder than the first time?........................................................

If this has changed, why do you think it has changed?

..............................................................................................................................

..............................................................................................................................

..............................................................................................................................

How would you like to improve it next time?

..............................................................................................................................

..............................................................................................................................

..............................................................................................................................

**THINK ABOUT...** WHAT HAS CHANGED | YOUR AIDS

## Stage three

Date .................................Session ................................................................

Did you find it easier or harder than the first time?........................................................

If this has changed, why do you think it has changed?

..............................................................................................................................
..............................................................................................................................
..............................................................................................................................

How would you like to improve it next time?

..............................................................................................................................
..............................................................................................................................
..............................................................................................................................

**NOTES**

..............................................................................................................................
..............................................................................................................................
..............................................................................................................................
..............................................................................................................................
..............................................................................................................................
..............................................................................................................................
..............................................................................................................................
..............................................................................................................................
..............................................................................................................................
..............................................................................................................................
..............................................................................................................................

| YOUR HORSE'S RESPONSE | YOUR HORSE'S WAY OF GOING

## CHAPTER SIX

# Compass

**CROSS • THIS WAY, THAT WAY • COMPASS**

This is another layout that's fantastic for when you want to practise dressage tests. Not only the lines, shapes and patterns, but also your transitions. Good transitions are well prepared, well balanced and well placed. The poles will guide your accuracy and they will also help to prepare your horse with the best possible balance and engagement to produce active, good-quality transitions.

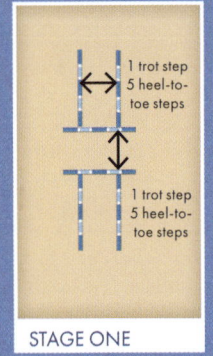

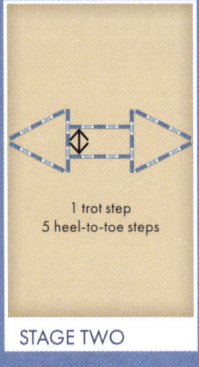

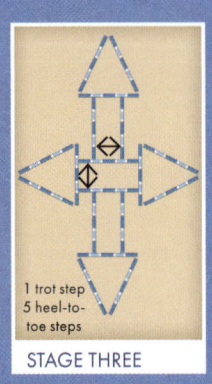

**STAGE ONE**
1 trot step
5 heel-to-toe steps

1 trot step
5 heel-to-toe steps

**STAGE TWO**
1 trot step
5 heel-to-toe steps

**STAGE THREE**
1 trot step
5 heel-to-toe steps

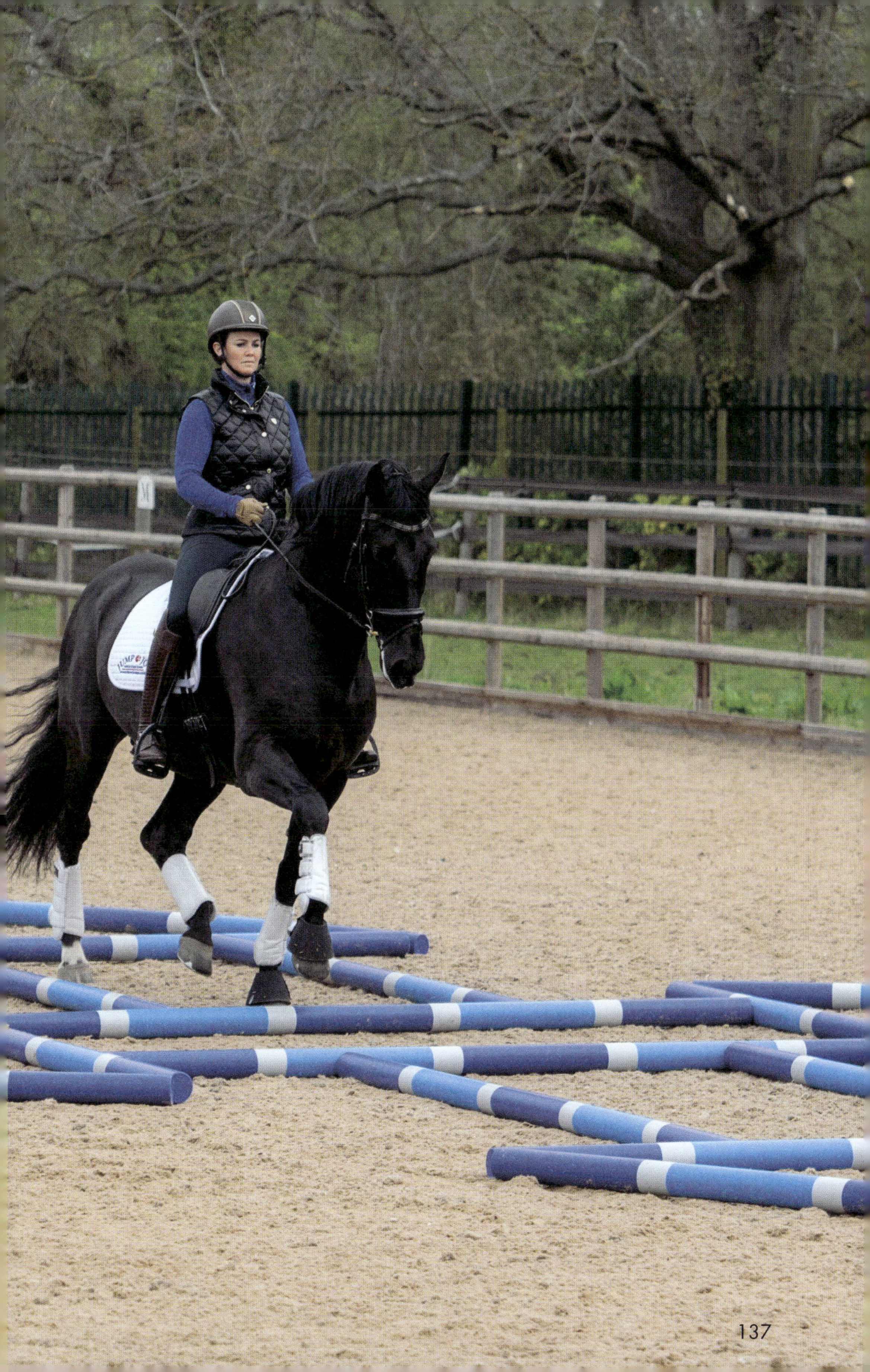

# THE CROSS
*Session one*

> **SET UP**
> Position this layout in the middle of the arena with X in the centre.

**THROUGH THE GAP**
Ride from E to B through the gap in walk, trot and canter, then level-up by trying some of these transitions...
- add in transitions either side, for example trot–walk–trot or canter–trot–canter
- add in transitions in the middle; for example, walk–canter, trot–halt–trot, trot–halt–rein-back–trot
- ride a flying change in the centre

It's very important to train straightness on this line right from the beginning, because at championships and higher levels, you will have a judge sitting at E/B.

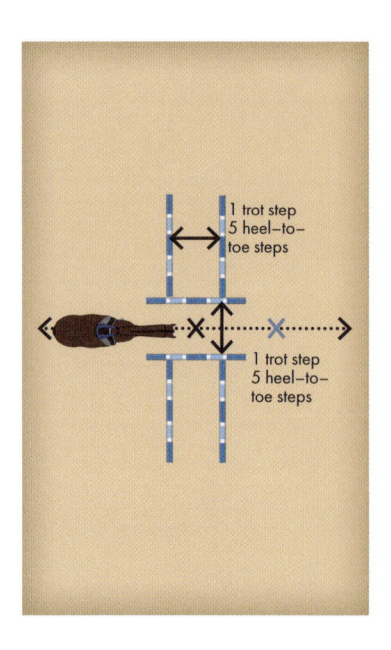

1 trot step
5 heel-to-toe steps

1 trot step
5 heel-to-toe steps

> **SESSION QUESTIONS: FIRST USE**

Date of writing in journal?......................................................................

How many times did you ride each exercise? ..........................................

How hard did you find the session?

😃    😐    😩

What did this session make you focus on most in terms of your aiding/riding?

................................................................................................................
................................................................................................................
................................................................................................................
................................................................................................................
................................................................................................................

138

Stage one

What did this session make you focus on most in terms of your horse's responses and way of going?
..................................................................................................
..................................................................................................
..................................................................................................
..................................................................................................

What would you most like to improve in your schooling for next time?
..................................................................................................
..................................................................................................
..................................................................................................
..................................................................................................

### SESSION QUESTIONS: FIRST USE

Date of writing in journal?......................................................................................

How many times did you ride each exercise? ..............................................

How hard did you find the session?

😃     😐     😥

What did this session make you focus on most in terms of your aiding/riding?

...................................................................................................................................

...................................................................................................................................

...................................................................................................................................

...................................................................................................................................

...................................................................................................................................

Stage one

# THE CROSS
*Session two*

**CENTRE LINE IN TROT**
Concentrate on riding your centre lines through the middle of the layout in trot, then try...
- trot with a halt in the tramline (black)
- trot with halt, rein back, trot in the tramline (blue)

The tramlines are particularly useful for monitoring and maintaining alignment in the rein-back. If your horse is going crooked, correct it with your seat. If they are going haunches right, they will be pushing your right hip forwards, so to correct it, bring your right hip back.

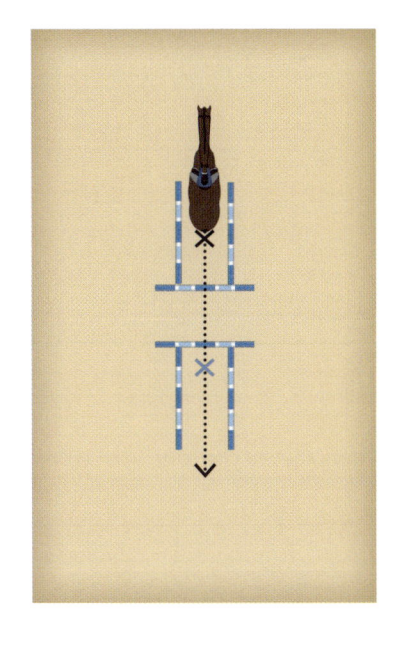

What did this session make you focus on most in terms of your horse's responses and way of going?

..................................................................................................................................
..................................................................................................................................
..................................................................................................................................
..................................................................................................................................

What would you most like to improve in your schooling for next time?

..................................................................................................................................
..................................................................................................................................
..................................................................................................................................
..................................................................................................................................

# THE CROSS
*Session three*

**CANTER–TROT–CANTER CENTRE LINE**
Initially, break the exercise down. Start by trotting through the first tramline and over the pair of poles, picking up canter in the second tramline.

Next, canter towards the poles, make a transition to trot in the first tramline and trot over the poles and out through the second tramline.

Finally, ride canter (red), trot (black), canter (red). Try it on both leads, picking up to the same lead again and with a change of lead.

## "Don't underestimate the difficulty of simple transitions performed well on a straight line"

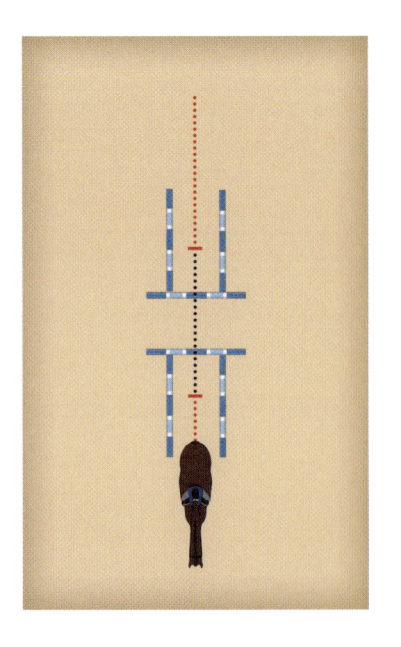

### SESSION QUESTIONS: FIRST USE

Date of writing in journal?......................................................................................

How many times did you ride each exercise? .......................................................

How hard did you find the session?

😀     😐     😥

What did this session make you focus on most in terms of your aiding/riding?

..............................................................................................................................
..............................................................................................................................
..............................................................................................................................
..............................................................................................................................
..............................................................................................................................

Stage one

What did this session make you focus on most in terms of your horse's responses and way of going?

..................................................................................................................................................
..................................................................................................................................................
..................................................................................................................................................
..................................................................................................................................................

What would you most like to improve in your schooling for next time?

..................................................................................................................................................
..................................................................................................................................................
..................................................................................................................................................
..................................................................................................................................................

Date ...................................................Session ................................................................

Did you find it easier or harder than the first time?................................................................

If this has changed, why do you think it has changed?

................................................................................................................................................

................................................................................................................................................

................................................................................................................................................

How would you like to improve it next time?

................................................................................................................................................

................................................................................................................................................

................................................................................................................................................

Date ...................................................Session ................................................................

Did you find it easier or harder than the first time?................................................................

If this has changed, why do you think it has changed?

................................................................................................................................................

................................................................................................................................................

................................................................................................................................................

How would you like to improve it next time?

................................................................................................................................................

................................................................................................................................................

................................................................................................................................................

**THINK ABOUT... WHAT HAS CHANGED | YOUR AIDS**

## Stage one

Date .................................................Session ........................................................................

Did you find it easier or harder than the first time?........................................................

If this has changed, why do you think it has changed?

................................................................................................................................

................................................................................................................................

................................................................................................................................

How would you like to improve it next time?

................................................................................................................................

................................................................................................................................

................................................................................................................................

**NOTES**

................................................................................................................................

................................................................................................................................

................................................................................................................................

................................................................................................................................

................................................................................................................................

................................................................................................................................

................................................................................................................................

................................................................................................................................

................................................................................................................................

................................................................................................................................

| YOUR HORSE'S RESPONSE | YOUR HORSE'S WAY OF GOING

# THIS WAY OR THAT?
*Session one*

> **SET UP**
> Position your poles so X is in the centre of the tramline and the triangles point towards E and B.

### E TO B IN WALK AND TROT
Walk and trot through the layout entering and exiting through the points of the triangles. Add in a halt transition in the tramline (blue cross). Focus on riding balanced turns on and off the long side so that you are straight when you are crossing the poles. Aim to keep your lines smooth and continuous.

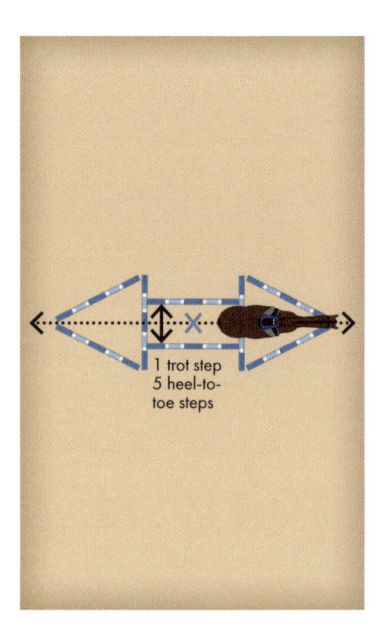

1 trot step
5 heel-to-toe steps

---

**SESSION QUESTIONS: FIRST USE**

Date of writing in journal?..........................................................................................

How many times did you ride each exercise? ............................................................

How hard did you find the session?

😀　😐　😩

What did this session make you focus on most in terms of your aiding/riding?

..................................................................................................................................

..................................................................................................................................

..................................................................................................................................

..................................................................................................................................

..................................................................................................................................

## Stage two

**What did this session make you focus on most in terms of your horse's responses and way of going?**

..................................................................................................................................
..................................................................................................................................
..................................................................................................................................
..................................................................................................................................

**What would you most like to improve in your schooling for next time?**

..................................................................................................................................
..................................................................................................................................
..................................................................................................................................
..................................................................................................................................

Loops are fantastic suppling and strengthening exercises, especially for young horses.

### SESSION QUESTIONS: FIRST USE

Date of writing in journal?......................................................................................

How many times did you ride each exercise? .............................................................

How hard did you find the session?

😃　　😐　　😩

What did this session make you focus on most in terms of your aiding/riding?

..................................................................................................................
..................................................................................................................
..................................................................................................................
..................................................................................................................
..................................................................................................................

Stage two

# THIS WAY OR THAT?
## Session two

**SHALLOW LOOPS**
Ride these loops on both reins equally and in both directions.

**Loop 1:** 10m over centre line. The line should be smooth and symmetrical either side of the poles. If you are in rising trot, you will need to change your diagonal as you cross the quarter line so you are one the correct diagonal for the new bend in the centre of the loop, then change it back the second time you cross the quarter line, ready for the corner.

**Loop 2:** ride the loop 7–8m over the triangle. The line should be smooth and symmetrical, crossing symmetrical stripes of the poles. Change your diagonal if you're rising to the trot, just as you did in the first exercise.

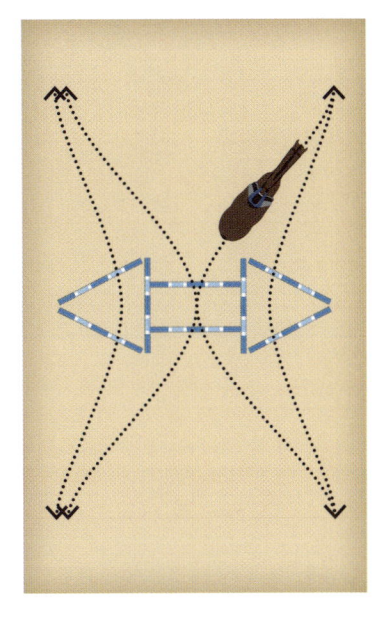

What did this session make you focus on most in terms of your horse's responses and way of going?

..................................................................................................................................
..................................................................................................................................
..................................................................................................................................
..................................................................................................................................

What would you most like to improve in your schooling for next time?

..................................................................................................................................
..................................................................................................................................
..................................................................................................................................
..................................................................................................................................

# THIS WAY OR THAT?

*Session three*

**COUNTER-CANTER LOOP**
This is a fairly advanced exercise, so focus on maintaining the correct position and bend in the counter-canter. Horses who are green in the counter-canter can often be a bit flat, but the poles will add plenty of lift and push.

Counter-canter is one of the most under-used, but most valuable, training exercises. It really allows you to access the muscles within your horse's ribcage and encourage suppleness – and, therefore, improve engagement.

If your horse is not balanced enough to counter-canter around the short side of the arena in preparation for this exercise, try striking off into counter-canter at the start of the loop and trotting at the end of it.

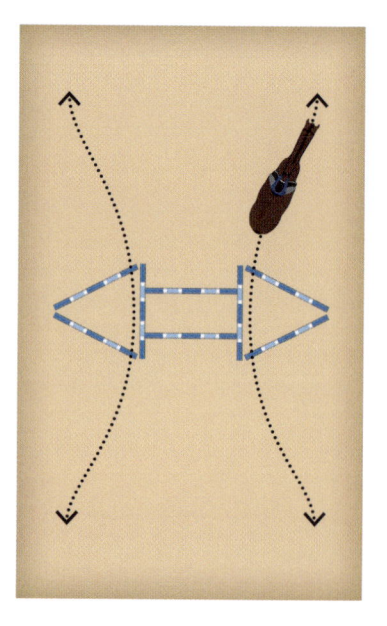

## SESSION QUESTIONS: FIRST USE

Date of writing in journal?....................................................

How many times did you ride each exercise? ....................................................

How hard did you find the session?

😀    😐    😫

What did this session make you focus on most in terms of your aiding/riding?

....................................................
....................................................
....................................................
....................................................

Stage two

What did this session make you focus on most in terms of your horse's responses and way of going?
..................................................................................................................................
..................................................................................................................................
..................................................................................................................................
..................................................................................................................................

What would you most like to improve in your schooling for next time?
..................................................................................................................................
..................................................................................................................................
..................................................................................................................................
..................................................................................................................................

Date .................................................Session ............................................................................

Did you find it easier or harder than the first time?.......................................................

If this has changed, why do you think it has changed?
................................................................................................................................
................................................................................................................................
................................................................................................................................

How would you like to improve it next time?
................................................................................................................................
................................................................................................................................
................................................................................................................................


Date .................................................Session ............................................................................

Did you find it easier or harder than the first time?.......................................................

If this has changed, why do you think it has changed?
................................................................................................................................
................................................................................................................................
................................................................................................................................

How would you like to improve it next time?
................................................................................................................................
................................................................................................................................
................................................................................................................................

**THINK ABOUT... WHAT HAS CHANGED | YOUR AIDS**

# Stage two

Date .................................................Session ...........................................................

Did you find it easier or harder than the first time?........................................................

If this has changed, why do you think it has changed?
..............................................................................................................................
..............................................................................................................................
..............................................................................................................................

How would you like to improve it next time?
..............................................................................................................................
..............................................................................................................................
..............................................................................................................................

**NOTES**

..............................................................................................................................
..............................................................................................................................
..............................................................................................................................
..............................................................................................................................
..............................................................................................................................
..............................................................................................................................
..............................................................................................................................
..............................................................................................................................
..............................................................................................................................
..............................................................................................................................
..............................................................................................................................

| YOUR HORSE'S RESPONSE | YOUR HORSE'S WAY OF GOING

# COMPASS
*Session one*

**SET UP**
Start in the middle of the arena so the triangles with the single tramline are pointing to E and B, and the double tramlines run along the centre line with the triangles pointing to A and C.

**CENTRE LINE IN TROT**
There are so many different ways you can ride through the centre of this layout it's easy to mix things up and also take your schooling to the next level. Focus on preparing your transitions and turns far enough in advance as you try some of these suggestions...
- ride a straight centre line
- make dogleg turns on and/or off the centre line. Try all variations and directions
- add in halts in the tramlines (red)
- ride a halt–rein-back–trot in the tramline (blue)

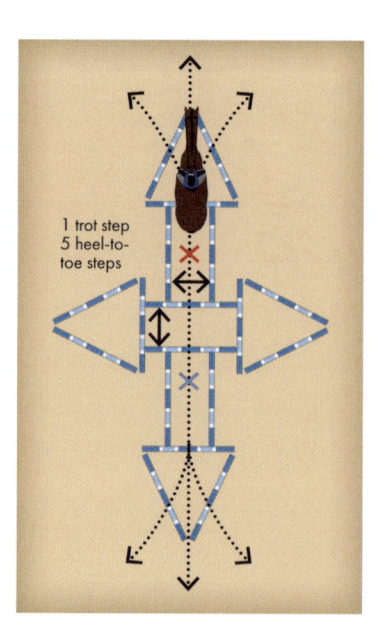

1 trot step
5 heel-to-toe steps

**SESSION QUESTIONS: FIRST USE**

Date of writing in journal?............................................................

How many times did you ride each exercise?.................................

How hard did you find the session?

😀    😐    😩

What did this session make you focus on most in terms of your aiding/riding?

..........................................................................................................
..........................................................................................................
..........................................................................................................
..........................................................................................................
..........................................................................................................

Stage three

What did this session make you focus on most in terms of your horse's responses and way of going?

..................................................................................................................

..................................................................................................................

..................................................................................................................

..................................................................................................................

What would you most like to improve in your schooling for next time?

..................................................................................................................

..................................................................................................................

..................................................................................................................

..................................................................................................................

### SESSION QUESTIONS: FIRST USE

Date of writing in journal?..................................................................................

How many times did you ride each exercise? ............................................................

How hard did you find the session?

😀     😐     😩

What did this session make you focus on most in terms of your aiding/riding?

..................................................................................................................

..................................................................................................................

..................................................................................................................

..................................................................................................................

..................................................................................................................

156

Stage three

# COMPASS
*Session two*

**20M CIRCLES**
- trot or canter through the single triangle (black)
- trot over the tramline (blue)
- trot or canter through triangle, tramline, triangle (red)

Use the poles as guides for symmetry, adding in transitions before and after the poles.

> "By now you have ridden many circle exercises over poles. Get creative and challenge yourself with transitions before and after the poles"

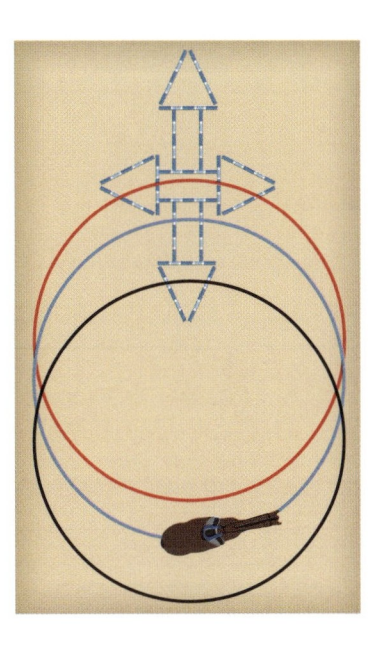

What did this session make you focus on most in terms of your horse's responses and way of going?

..................................................................................................................................................
..................................................................................................................................................
..................................................................................................................................................
..................................................................................................................................................

What would you most like to improve in your schooling for next time?

..................................................................................................................................................
..................................................................................................................................................
..................................................................................................................................................
..................................................................................................................................................

# COMPASS
*Session three*

**CIRCLES OF FULL FIGURE OF EIGHT**
Use the poles as a guide for symmetry when changing from one circle to the next.
**Level 1**: ride the entire layout in trot
**Level 2**: transitions either side of the poles, trot–walk–trot
**Level 3**: transitions either side of the poles, canter–trot–canter

Often, when transitions are added, the line changes, so use the poles to monitor and maintain symmetry of the line.

> "So many riders lose accuracy on two half-20m circles. With the poles, it really makes you notice where the line should be"

## SESSION QUESTIONS: FIRST USE

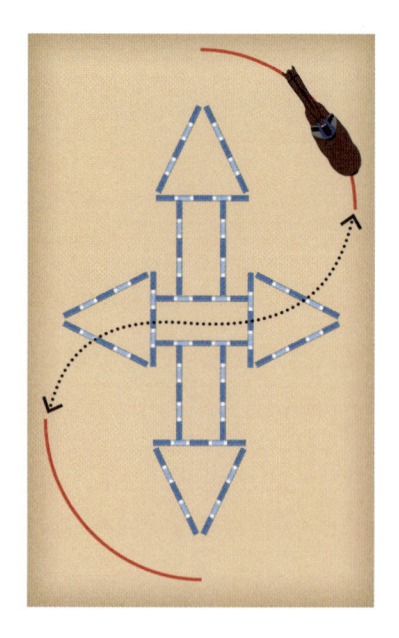

Date of writing in journal?......................................................................

How many times did you ride each exercise? ................................................

How hard did you find the session?

😃   😐   😩

What did this session make you focus on most in terms of your aiding/riding?

..........................................................................................................
..........................................................................................................
..........................................................................................................
..........................................................................................................

158

Stage three

What did this session make you focus on most in terms of your horse's responses and way of going?
..................................................................................................................................................
..................................................................................................................................................
..................................................................................................................................................
..................................................................................................................................................

What would you most like to improve in your schooling for next time?
..................................................................................................................................................
..................................................................................................................................................
..................................................................................................................................................
..................................................................................................................................................

Date ................................................Session ......................................................................

Did you find it easier or harder than the first time?......................................................

If this has changed, why do you think it has changed?

................................................................................................................................

................................................................................................................................

................................................................................................................................

How would you like to improve it next time?

................................................................................................................................

................................................................................................................................

................................................................................................................................

Date ................................................Session ......................................................................

Did you find it easier or harder than the first time?......................................................

If this has changed, why do you think it has changed?

................................................................................................................................

................................................................................................................................

................................................................................................................................

How would you like to improve it next time?

................................................................................................................................

................................................................................................................................

................................................................................................................................

**THINK ABOUT... WHAT HAS CHANGED | YOUR AIDS**

# Stage three

Date .................................Session ..........................................................

Did you find it easier or harder than the first time?........................................................

If this has changed, why do you think it has changed?
..................................................................................................................
..................................................................................................................
..................................................................................................................

How would you like to improve it next time?
..................................................................................................................
..................................................................................................................
..................................................................................................................

**NOTES**

..................................................................................................................
..................................................................................................................
..................................................................................................................
..................................................................................................................
..................................................................................................................
..................................................................................................................
..................................................................................................................
..................................................................................................................
..................................................................................................................
..................................................................................................................
..................................................................................................................

| YOUR HORSE'S RESPONSE | YOUR HORSE'S WAY OF GOING

# HOW DID YOU GET ON?

Which was your favourite series?..................................................................

Why?..........................................................................................................

....................................................................................................................

....................................................................................................................

Which specific exercise was your favourite?..................................................

Why?..........................................................................................................

....................................................................................................................

....................................................................................................................

What do you feel has improved most in terms of your riding?

....................................................................................................................

....................................................................................................................

....................................................................................................................

What do you feel has improved most in terms of your horse's way of going?

....................................................................................................................

....................................................................................................................

....................................................................................................................

Do you plan to continue to use polework in your training? ...........................

How? ........................................................................................................

....................................................................................................................

....................................................................................................................

....................................................................................................................